Peter Roebuck opens for Somerset. He is, therefore, a dressing room colleague of Richards, Botham and Garner and is in an almost unique position as a leading cricket writer while still playing in the first-class game.

It Never Rains is an account of one first-class cricketer's progress through a season, with an analysis of how his own state of mind varied according to his own and his team's success or failure. Never before has cricket's ability to generate personal elation and gloom been so graphically described.

The season in question had plenty of both as the Somerset side took the NatWest Bank Trophy and came second in the John Player League only on a technicality. The other, non-glamorous side of the professional cricketer's life is the effort to whip up enthusiasm on a cold, September afternoon; the interminable cross-country drives; the succession of soulless hotel rooms; the inevitable tensions in a party thrown together away from home.

For Peter Roebuck, the search for perfection is the justification for playing cricket, yet he is clear-sighted enough to know that perfection cannot be attained and he describes with honesty and sensitivity this dilemma, his efforts to resolve it, and how it affected his state of mind throughout the season.

D1637606

IT NEVER RAINS

RAINS

A CRICKETER'S LOT

Peter Roebuck

Illustrated by Mike Tarr

London
UNWIN PAPERBACKS
Boston   Sydney

First published in Great Britain by George Allen & Unwin 1984
First published by Unwin Paperbacks 1985

UNWIN®PAPERBACKS
40 Museum Street, London WC1A 1LU, UK

Unwin Paperbacks
Park Lane, Hemel Hempstead, Herts HP2 4TE, UK

George Allen & Unwin Australia Pty Ltd
8 Napier Street, North Sydney, NSW 2060, Australia

British Library Cataloguing in Publication Data

Roebuck, Peter, 1956–
It never rains : a cricketer's lot.
1. Roebuck, Peter, 1956– 2. Cricket players—
England—Biography
I. Title
796.35'8'0924   GV915.R6/
ISBN 0-04-796096-5

Set in Plantin by A. J. Latham Ltd, Dunstable
and printed in Great Britain
by Guernsey Press Co. Ltd Guernsey, Channel Islands

Contents

Preface   *page* vii
1. A Dry Game in a Wet Land   1
2. A Duck and a Swipe   19
3. Up and Down, In and Out   39
4. I Am a Captain   61
5. A Hundred At Last – Nearly Two   83
6. A Low on the Road   100
7. Towards a Semi-Final   112
8. Trench Warfare   126
9. Bang and a Whimper   138

For:
Julia
Nicholas
Toby
Griffo

Preface

It was after reading David Foot's extraordinary book, *Harold Gimblett: a tormented genius*, that I decided to describe the experiences of this county cricketer. I'm not a genius nor tormented — well, not much — but it struck me that Foot's book gave an accurate impression of what it must have been like to play professional cricket 30 years ago. In *It Never Rains . . .* I have tried to be as honest as possible in relating my experiences as a county cricketer in 1983. We must, though, always remember Ambrose Bierce's warning: '*Diary*: A daily record of that part of one's life which one can relate to oneself without blushing.'

No doubt I've ignored many embarrassing things; for example, reading through this record, I note I scarcely mention my batting average, yet it was at the back of my mind throughout the season. But I hope I've not ducked all the challenges and I hope that you will find here an account of the laughter and melancholy that have decorated these months. As with *Slices of Cricket* you will not find much of sex, violence, drugs and booze within these pages. Probably you will suspect, as must a dog surveying a bone, that all the best bits have been taken away. I leave out that side of professional sport because it does not interest me much. It is the individual battles I find fascinating and it is those, set against the background, that I have tried to describe here.

Finally I must thank Mike Tarr for his illustrations, John Newth for his editing and encouragement and Sandra for her patient typing. I must also mention Sam's bacon butties. To my horror I see that I've omitted any mention of bacon butties in these pages, but they were there whenever I drove into the County Ground late at night after a long away trip.

1

A Dry Game in a Wet Land

Tuesday 5 April

Well, here we are, three days after a 13,000-mile journey from
Sydney, back at work. This will be my tenth season as a
professional.

It all started most unpromisingly. We met in the staff room
at Millfield School, renewing old friendships, meeting new
players and gruffly acknowledging people we were only half
pleased to see. Eventually speeches were made and we sipped
tea and after about half an hour the brief prelude was over. We
collected our bags from our cars and headed towards the
changing rooms. We're spending our first week at Millfield
because it has such a wide range of facilities, and then we'll be
back to Taunton and hopefully some outdoor nets. This week

will be mainly a matter of warming up, a reminder of the days when cricketers spent their winters sipping pints and downing bowls of Christmas pudding. I'm fit enough, I've been training with some Rugby players down under, and anyway I think one builds up stamina during the season. I can't see any sense in charging about, burning up precious energy, on muddy rugby fields on 6 April.

Of course, I didn't actually say that to our trainer but ran dolefully along at the back like some ageing Austin in a field of sleek Capris. Colin Dredge accompanied me; he's a semi-professional soccer player and has no need to train at all. We grunted and wailed, which we thought might indicate sufficient agony to keep our trainer happy for a day.

Nevertheless, I feel poorly this evening. I don't think it was the training nor the sweeping rain. It was the fruit cocktail I ate in Bombay airport. How could I be so foolish as to eat a tinned fruit cocktail in Bombay airport?

Wednesday 6 April

The way things are going, this could be the shortest, dullest diary ever. Today I'm ill and didn't go to work — does 'work' sound okay? I collapsed into bed at 7.30 last night and lurking black clouds this morning encouraged me to stay there.

I'll tell you a bit more about yesterday. After all, it was the first day of a new season for a successful, professional cricket team. Our routine was vague. Cricketers are, in the main, reluctant to train or practise specifically for cricket. Our concept of training is to stretch some muscles, sprint a few sprints, go for a run if we have to and end up with a fiercely fought soccer game in which someone is usually injured. We do very little repetitive practice designed to master our craft. In the nets we strap on our pads, biff a ball about and pronounce ourselves 'in form'. I don't think gymnasts, snooker players or golfers are so prepared to put themselves in the laps of the Gods. Their approach is carefully disciplined, they examine and re-examine their technique. Compared to them we are astonishingly amateurish. In fact, most of us were technically better at 14 than we are now. We score more runs, of course, because we have accumulated the confidence and experience to collect runs against fast bowling supported by a cordon of slips on a doubtful pitch. That is the primary experience of modern batsmanship.

And yet perhaps it is not fair to compare cricket with these other sports. Old Bill Alley could work on his farm all winter, turn up in April and his first ball in six months would inevitably land on a threepenny bit. Unlike snooker and golf, cricket is a game of movement, a game reliant as much upon rhythm and determination as upon technique. Plenty of people can reproduce shots accurately and still fail. Plenty of people can hardly play a shot of all and succeed. Take Peter Denning as an example. If he worried about all the things he can't do, he'd never score a run. He can't drive on the leg-side. He can't hit straight. He isn't good at hooking. And he isn't able to dance down the pitch either. What he can do is play within his limitations, battle on with guts and courage and score lots of runs when you need them.

Perhaps cricket is more like boxing than any other sport in the way is transcends mere technical mastery and requires hidden gifts of timing and judgement as well as strength of character.

Thursday 7 April

Passed a quiet day in bed (it's been a triumph so far this season, hasn't it?), reading David Foot's moving biography of Harold Gimblett. I knew Gimblett at Millfield School where he ran the sports shop and joined in the coaching. He was a strange but kindly man who lived a most self-contained life. I played against him once. He must have been over 50 and I can still recall a graceful drive he played through mid-wicket to the ropes. He scored, I suppose, about 21. I can't really remember. But that one shot had the economical power of true excellence.

It's a sad tale about a complex man. Gimblett felt all of the taxing insecurity of cricket, only he felt it more strongly than anyone else. He took his own life in 1978, a reed broken by the wind. Before his death he had rung Foot and told him he wanted to write his book so that the public 'can know what it's really like being a professional sportsman when you are a worrier'.

This game preys on doubt. It is a precarious game. Form, luck, confidence are transitory things. It's never easy to work out why they have so inexplicably deserted you. Inevitably you analyse, you fret, you try to understand what's happened. Why was the game so easy yesterday? Why is it so impossible today? Sometimes you condemn yourself, as if it were your fault that your drive ends up in gully's hands, that your bat will not swing through straight. Sometimes you tense yourself to try harder, sometimes you decide to relax and to go for your shots. Probably neither works. As Foot says, 'Cricket is played very much with the mind. Only the unimaginative player escapes the tension. Many, whatever their seeming unconcern, retreat into caverns of introspection.'

It is a cussed game. It can show you glimpses of beauty in a stroke perfectly played, perhaps, and then it throws you back into the trough of mediocrity. Only the most phlegmatic or those who don't give a damn or those with unshakeable belief survive these upheavals easily. Gimblett must have torn himself with worry. He must have twisted himself into rejection, not only of his own personality but of people around him, too. He must have sensed envy and plots; suspicions of others must have burdened him as he sought some explanation for his failures.

Usually the good times return – Gimblett had a magnificent career – but there is no guarantee, that is the worst of it. Why should runs ever return? You are trying hard, the pitches are good, the bowling only fair. There is no rational reason for failure, nor any rational reason why fortune's wind should change. Maybe cricketers 'shouldn't take it so personal' but most of us do all the same.

In this light it's strange that cricket attracts so many insecure men. It is surely the very worst game for an intense character, yet it continues to find many obtuse sensitivities amongst its players. Men of imagination, men of ideals risk its harsh exposures. There must be some fascinating stimulation in the game to make so many of us, so ill-prepared for turmoil, risk its ugly changes. Otherwise we'd never tolerate its bounce of failure. And it is mostly failure, even for the best.

Yes, a remarkable book, that Gimblett book. It reminded me of patches of my own life and my career which I'd far rather forget, times when ill fortune or sheer bad play caused me first to tear myself to pieces and then to turn on my undeserving friends.

Friday 8 April

Rose heroically from my sick-bed this evening to have a bat against my brother in the nets. Pretty awful. Can't quite work out how to bat this season. Always before, I've stood still and blocked the ball. Today I tried to get more behind it by moving before the ball was bowled. If this works it would help me to avoid edging the ball so often.

Trouble is, it doesn't work for me somehow. I don't know how Boycott and the rest do it so well, this back and across thing. Whenever I try it, I end up off-balance and playing across the line with my head tilting towards gully.

There must be an answer. Scrutinising things, if I can get in behind the ball I should be able to hit it more often. Good players appear to arrive in the right place at the right time as if it were the most natural thing in the world. They are always balanced and in command of the ball, always playing the ball near to their bodies. How do they do it? They play very late. Apart from that, you can't really generalise about excellent batsmen.

I must try to iron out my weaknesses before May (if you could see my ironing you would think my choice of verb unfortunate). In cricket you have to try always to move either to the line of the ball or according to its length. Most opening batsmen choose their shot depending upon the line of the ball in relation to the stumps. Men like Edrich, Lawry, Boycott leave alone as many balls as possible early in their innings.

On the other hand, most middle-order batsmen want to hit the ball. They let far fewer deliveries pass, they want to dominate the bowlers. Their stroke is determined by the length of the ball. Can they drive or pull? If not, they may settle for defence. The line of the ball is much less relevant, and wide long-hops are not wasted.

For nine years I've concentrated on playing forward and hoping to drive. Opening last year for the first time, I found this meant I played at far too many balls, encouraging the bowlers to bowl wide to entice slip catches. Whether or not by moving back and across before each ball, if I'm opening this season, I must be more in control of my shots and stop playing those dreadful twiddly things outside the off stump. Make the buggers bowl straight.

Oh well. It's we cricketers who make this confoundedly simple game difficult. Griffo, a friend of mine in Sydney, listened to my advice as to how to coach his lowly cricket team. He tried a few practices and watched a match. He returned to say that his team didn't hit the ball hard enough, they just patted it here and there in a timid manner. Griffo's sole instruction thereafter was to 'hit the thing harder and more often'.

He could be right. Anyhow, one thing's for sure. This season I'm going to pick up the bat higher and swing it with a little less reluctance.

Do you think this resolution will last the month? Shake not thy gory locks at me! You don't think I'll go back to all that tried and trusted poking around, do you? Trouble is, I'm only happy when I'm fighting things out. I don't play cricket in a relaxed and enjoyable way — it's the growling and tension I like about what is otherwise an utterly ridiculous game.

One more thing: Skipper Rose says he's going to give the youngsters a chance this year. That doesn't sound too good, does it?

I used to be a young 'un but in cricket when you've been around for a few years you immediately become a veteran. There is no intervening noun, it's an overnight experience. One minute you are 'up and coming', the next 'a wily old pro'.

Monday 11 April

Wet. Cold. Bleak. Sleet. 'Orrible. Back to work. It was a pleasant weekend, and my horse won the Grand National. Is this a sign of a lucky summer? No, of course it bloody well isn't!

Drove to work in my brand-new sponsored car. We cricketers are terribly cushioned. I haven't bought a car for five years, not in England at any rate. (I did buy a $200 thing in Sydney, but I can't call it a car since I imagine the word connotes some mechanical quality entirely absent in that heap of metal.) Most of our meals are free or paid for from generous expenses and my kit comes free, too. I even get my haircuts in

Taunton for nothing. This cushion pushes cricketers into a self-important world for six months. For six months many of us will be only half aware of the realities of most people's lives. We'll drive our cars, eat our steaks, arrive at the ground to fend off autograph hunters and bumpers with equal determination and generally show ourselves only in areas where we are the pampered stars. We'll forget how unimportant we are in most people's lives unless our wives kick us or friends outside cricket show not one bit of interest in our affairs.

Shortly after my return to work this morning I sustained a blow on my finger from a lifter in the indoor nets bowled by G. Palmer. I developed a large blood blister. It's been a lovely start to the season.

Moreover I batted poorly. As usual, my drives all screwed through square leg like some hack golfer. Put a bloke there and I'm out of business.

To add to my sense of horror, I saw a sheet which listed my last season's dismissals. Apparently I was bowled a mere five times, lbw only four times, stumped twice and caught 36 times! 36!! If I hit the ball on the ground, they'd never get me out.

Most of those catches were from shots aimed through point. My bat twists either too far or not far enough when I play that shot. I've never been very good at it (there was a shed in the covers in my back yard at home and no runs were available that way). In the past I've not tried to play that shot much. If I stick to the shots I'm good at, I'll score more runs. Trouble is, all the other teams know exactly which shots I'm good at, and they bowl a good length on off stump to me. I must find an answer.

With quickies, I simply have to leave the ball alone and, if they are happy wasting the new ball, so be it. With spinners it's more difficult. If I avoid trying to hit the ball through cover point, what shall I do with it? Can't just ignore it. By the time the spinners are on I ought to be trying to dominate. I'll just have to attack them. Ken McEwan, who has a reputation as a prodigious hitter of spinners, says he only started clobbering slow bowlers because he didn't think he could play them normally. Anyway I've decided to refuse to be intimidated by left-arm spinners. It was absurd last year that I was dreading the opposition captain putting on the left-arm spinner. Good God, I was hoping they'd leave on Malcolm Marshall and not bring on John Southern – not a view shared by many batsmen. It's stupid to tolerate this weakness. If I can't play them in a classical way, I wonder if I can fool the captains. If I whack them a couple of times, they might think I'm a superb player of spinners, mightn't they?

I told our coach that I had decided to hit out at left-arm spinners this year. I think this probably ruined his day. It might brighten up the season a bit, though.

This morning, Skipper Rose appointed Popplewell in charge of training. I announced that this was the most disastrous appointment ever. Popplewell is a fitness fanatic. We'll be hunting across wetlands, through hidden lanes, doing press-ups in sheds and sprinting in farmyards and all the while Nigel will be swearing at us. He only swears because all trainers swear and because he suspects that some of us wouldn't run fast unless someone was swearing.

As a matter of fact, I didn't run too badly today. Sixth out of, oh, twelve at least. Wasn't so good at the piggy-back races, though. The relation between piggy-backs and fending off Imran Khan was a little too remote for me to grasp.

Tuesday 12 April

I spent most of the day in Birmingham, attending our Cricketers' Association meeting. John Arlott is our President and has taken to making superbly crusty speeches, a sort of wined Solzhenitsyn of cricket. Under his guidance our debates are always fair, with each speech heard in silence, however outrageous (and Boycott has spoken).

Before lunch we had a rather solemn debate about the state of English cricket. Everyone seems worried about the state of English everything. No-one knew what to do about it, or at least everyone knew what to do but no-one could agree on anything. Four-day cricket? Leagues? Fewer overseas players? Better pitches? Many ideas were mooted. The best of them was the league idea put by Phil Carrick, who brought the house down by waving his piece of paper as if he was Neville Chamberlain and beginning, 'Last Tuesday all the Yorkshire players met and we all agreed' etc. He has to make this same start at every meeting and we wait for it as eagerly as *Navy*

Lark fans awaiting Lieutenant Phillips' 'left hand down a bit'. All of Yorkshire's ideas bore a marked resemblance to ideas put forward by Raymond Illingworth a few weeks ago.

Fortunately there was beer for lunch and after that things brightened up a bit. Apparently they want to stop all the appeals. Last year they wanted to stop us changing our trousers if they split. They suggested that only 'keeper, slip and bowler be allowed to appeal. John Arlott thought it was a splendid idea as it might improve the Australians. We said it was silly, that the pressures on umpires in county games were not too great and that if there was something wrong with Test cricket, it ought to sort it out itself.

I managed to add to the merriment by making a brief contribution along the lines that 'People didn't cheat in county cricket' . . . (pause for consideration) . . . 'much'.

Yes, a cheerful day, but embarrassing, too. With all these county cricketers around (all the new black fast bowlers, all the youngsters I couldn't recognise), you wonder if anyone knows who you are and what they think of you. Do you say, 'There's that bloke Roebuck who can't bat' or 'Isn't that old Roebuck over there, that fine professional batsman whom we all respect so much?' It is important to be held in high esteem by your professional peers.

11 pm.   Just finished a three-hour batting lesson from Hallam Moseley, our bespectacled no. 11. Do you find something slightly odd about that? Hallam has been doing an advanced coaching course and says he's learnt a lot. He says he's going to put it into practice, except that he doesn't think he'll be able to resist the occasional swipe (which is scarcely a strong enough word to capture that mighty flailing of arms and legs). He confided, 'I like to hit the ball too much, you know.'

He also made the disturbing comment that my new Duncan Fearnley bat looks good and that I should improve as it has stronger edges.

Wednesday 13 April

Went in early this morning (9 am) to practise on the club's new ball machine. It's a strange contraption with splints and what appear to be tyres whirling around. It shoots the ball out without warning so that if you put it on high speed you feel like a coconut. I want to use it to help groove my drives so that I can reproduce the same drive ball after ball. This way I'll be able to drive more boldly in a match, I hope. That's the advantage of the machine: it will land the ball in the same place nearly every time so that you can work on one fault. I haven't been able to do that since I was 13, when I used to practise with a ball in a sock dangling from a tree.

In 20 minutes I'd faced 150 balls. Gradually more ended up past the bowler. It was hard work (up, down, up, down) but I want to do it every morning before the season. Apart from improving the mechanics, it will help sharpen my mind. The brain blurs during the winter in Australia and returns in a docile, amiable mood, out of tune with the thankless competition of professional sport.

Also, the machine will encourage discipline. To me, cricket is a battle with the self; whenever I bat I feel ridiculous temptations I must restrain. The season is a five-month fight to play only strokes that are intelligently calculated. Others regard batting as a duel between bat and ball in which no favours are asked. This reflects the temperaments of these people – Close, Richards, Popplewell, Bairstow, for example – natural fighters who are in it for the confrontation rather than for self-discipline.

In the blur of winter I tend to reflect upon past seasons and make vows for the next. I look at my batting and see how to improve it. The trouble is, you forget the insecurities which are responsible for your physical weaknesses. It is doubt, not inability, which explains my cramped style. Take that stuff last week about lifting the bat higher and clouting left-arm spinners. Will it last? Is it realistic? Will it survive a couple of failures? Will I, my place under pressure, return to the safe pastures of introspective defence? We shall see.

Thursday 14 April

Vic's back! Found him in the dressing room after my half-hour on the ball machine. My old mate of 14 years has been on holiday with his wife, daughter and dog in Penzance, re-covering from his winter tour. No sign of Botham yet, and Richards and Garner are still playing Test cricket in the West Indies.

Vic hasn't changed since his tour to Australia; he's still bearded, gentle and slightly exasperated. Vic is my closest friend in cricket, my closest friend in England. (I'm only here six months of the year and I spend most of that in hotels and cars.) Over the years we've shared rooms, journeys, pizzas and games of golf. We laugh at the same things, or nearly — I laugh at him and he at me. We've seen each other rise and fall, shared many disappointments and some triumphs. He's a sponge that absorbs my upheavals but it isn't entirely one-way traffic. He's a fine cricketer, too, in his rural way. Maybe he's more of a rusty tractor than a new Maestro, and when he's out of form he can be dreadful; if he's out of touch he appears to be not so much watching the ball as looking for it. But he contributes a great deal to the team over the year. Mind you, he's a little accident-prone and subject to bouts of bewildering failure which help sharpen his humour. At Street a few years ago, we read our stars just for the hell of it and his said, 'Your judgement will be reliable today.' An hour later, he'd run three of us out.

What else? Well the daily grind continues. We trained hard again today with the usual stretches, long run and a series of sprints. As well, we sat around, I had two baths, five cups of coffee and two cups of tea. Home at 4 pm after an indoor net and then cooking and reading.

Friday 15 April

After two weeks of wind and showers, a reluctant sun peeped from behind clusters of white clouds, encouraging us to rush out to risk some outdoor cricket for the first time. Our grass nets are still muddy so we concentrated on a long fielding practice.

Sir Len Hutton has said that in his day fielding practice consisted of someone hitting the ball in the air to see if anyone caught it. Ten years ago Somerset fielding practices meant a game of soccer. Now we not only train hard (I'm very tired this evening) but also endure long sessions of catching, chasing and throwing. The importance of agility in the field has risen with the growing seriousness of the Sunday League. 40-over matches are not long enough to separate the good and the bad, and many are decided by a few runs here or there; if your team can just stop things rather than just missing them, you can sneak home in these matches. So there are many fewer Milburns around, fewer odd shapes and sizes in the game. Perhaps it's one of cricket's greatest attractions that, life golf, almost anybody could play it if the mind were willing. That is no longer so. A plump youngster needs to be substantially better than a rival if he is to succeed.

What's more, this need for mobility is causing men to retire earlier, chastened by embarrassment in front of baying thousands on Sundays. Of course, the top-quality cricketers — Alan Jones, Boycott, Illingworth, Hampshire, Gifford, Simmons etc — are remarkably fit, cunning enough to hide their weaknesses or worth their places anyway. But lesser men are hurried out of the game by their track-suited, eager and physically hard replacements.

Certainly our training regime is stern this year, with Popplewell charging around in his determinedly filthy tracksuit and the rest of us in his wake. Some of us are still huffing and puffing at the back — Denning, Marks, Roebuck, Dredge, Gard, people whose places are pretty secure. Botham does not train at all here. He is immensely strong and willing to tolerate a tough training scheme at Scunthorpe but can see no sense at all in it for cricket. Perhaps this is what frustrates purists about Botham. They cannot hold him up as a shining example. They can say that Boycott practises all the time and you must copy him. They can say that Gavaskar concentrates totally and you must copy him. They can say that Willis is wonderfully fit and a man to be copied. But of Botham, what can be said? He is huge, bold, laughing and sometimes reckless. Maybe he is the real man to follow, but it would be hard to persuade the Puritans of that.

I went to work early this morning for another 150 balls on the machine. My drive is improving, as it ruddy well ought to be.

The weekend is here. We have our first friendly on Monday without having had an outdoor net. It'll probably rain. I see that according to our fixture list, from 27 April our programme is heavy with only 26 days without first-class cricket until 15 September. And no doubt there will be ten benefit games on those days. It is going to be as much an endurance test as a test of skill.

Monday 18 April

It was a dry weekend, so we ought to have guessed. It started raining at five to nine and a mean drizzle continued until lunch. Our game against Glamorgan was abandoned, but not before they turned up with a new captain who looked like Dr Who, so festooned was he with scarves and trenchcoats and hair. But it turned out to be Mike Selvey, who has gone up the M4 to risk the unequal struggle.

I had my 150 balls on the machine instead of my first innings of the season. People are beginning to say they've never known it wetter.

With our match abandoned, we trundled off to a rugby field and did some training under Popplewell, who is fast affecting the healthy ruddiness of a cornflakes advert. He made us stretch our muscles 'until it burns', during which Hallam Moseley succeeded in stretching his legs without bending them and putting his chin on the ground. Try that! Then we gasped our way through a pyramid of sprints (25-yard sprints up to seven times without stopping, and then back down to one) followed by 12 lengths of the rugby field. The gnarled old pros were well to the rear by this stage. Our only ray of hope was the sight of the soccer ball which had been brought along. We did play soccer and Jeremy Lloyds went in the fetlock chasing the ball.

I'm afraid that 'gone in the fetlock' is the only medical term in my vocabulary and it will have to do for all injuries. With cars, by the way, the only diagnosis I know is 'the big end's gone'.

After the soccer we had a pleasantly long lunch, musing over funny times in the past. We rounded off the day with a 2½-hour indoor net session and I played well for the first time this season. It seems as if the cricket is creeping up on us and we've scarcely had a practice. Whoever started this game in England? A dry game in a wet land!

Tuesday 19 April

At 2.15 on the twelfth day of the season I faced my first ball on a grass pitch. Frankly I think our fortnight's training until today has been of little use. Too much physical work reduces our fluency in afternoon practices, and indoor nets tend to encourage lazy footwork because the ball does not deviate.

I played okay but am still collapsing my left elbow much too early; that's forced on me by my left foot edging too close to the ball, preventing a full and free swing. Square leg was still busy collecting my off-drives. I hit the ball harder than last year, either because of greater strength from an active winter or because I've changed from jumbos to Duncan Fearnley bats this year. I chose two bats from Duncan's factory and the one I'm using has a soft surface but plenty of meat. It's light, considering the amount of wood in it. My No. 2 bat has a resounding middle but a hollow bottom and I'll try to use it only in nets. I find it very important to grow into a bat and gloves and pads and even thigh-pad. When I use someone else's gear, it all feels strange and wrong.

Everyone had a net. Some tried to hit the ball into the river, others scarcely played a shot at all, trying to build up concentration (Wessels used to block every ball in the nets). I tried to make myself bat as I would in a match, as if I only had one chance, but I suspect my memory of how I bat in a match was very optimistic.

I suppose the aim of practice is to build up concentration so that batting becomes natural and you become absorbed in it. Whenever I see Boycott bat, it seems as if he barely concentrates at all but is absolutely absorbed in what he's doing. He is not Boycott holding a bat, but a batsman − as if he were a Stanislavsky actor.

As Rose and I sat in the warmth of the dressing room wondering how long we could desert our cold troops practising their fielding, he asked me whether I wanted to open this year. My first sustained experience as an opener was last year and it was only a partial success. I started opening partly because it secured my place in the Somerset team − there were no other people willing and able to open in Championship cricket except some youngsters − and partly because there were hardly any openers in England and it was my only chance of representing my country. Mind you, I'm not certain that deep down I want to represent my country. Not everyone does. It is obvious to me that I either want to play for England too much or not at all. How else can I explain several total collapses of form when people begin to speculate that my chance is bound to come soon? Am I too excited or too fearful? I can remember a benefit game last year when, as I was walking out to bat, I heard a spectator say to his son, 'There goes England's next opener.' I remember thinking, 'Oh no, don't say that.' Because it was something I desperately wanted? Or because I didn't relish the harsh exposure of a Test match?

Wednesday 20 April

It rained all day. Quite frankly, it's hard to see how any of us are going to play cricket this year.

We had a game of soccer and Denning went in the fetlock. He shouldn't have been playing but wanted to prove to Rose his full recovery from a knee injury so that he could play in our first match at Oxford. Hallam Moseley's shoulder is sore, and no-one seems to know what's wrong with it. And young Adrian Dunning is still suffering from a bad setting of a broken finger and can't hold a bat. All three must be wondering if they'll play first-class cricket again. These injuries can strike you at any stage of your career, adding to the risks of the game.

We had a brief meeting about expenses. Money is rarely mentioned in our dressing room. Apart from anything else, everyone is paid different amounts by the club and those paid the most like to disguise this. Only a few of our players are strongly motivated by money. Most of us came into the game because, well, we'd always wanted to. Marks, Botham and I started on £15 a week in 1974, which deterred us not one jot. Marks and I have Oxbridge degrees which might appear to give us a choice of profession except that neither of us had any intention of being deflected from our course by mere intelligence. We wanted to be cricketers even in those dark days of the 1960s when the game was so run down that my parents, intending to change my ambition before it settled, took me along to my first indoor net in Bath in the hope that I'd be hit by a hard cricket ball and put off the game for life. Or so they say! We carry on struggling, through habit I suppose, and though it is terrific to have a respectable wage, money is not even now all that important.

Thursday 21 April

Bumped into Gordon Prossor, our groundsman, this morning.
He shook his head over the weather and said 'Terrible, isn't it?
Terrible' which is the sort of thing you like to hear when you
are 63 for 7. It never rains when you want it to. Despite this,
we managed to have an outdoor net on a recently laid artificial
strip this afternoon.

In six days time we play our opening first-class fixture at
Oxford. So far we have had one net and already Denning,
Moseley and Lloyds have been lost. Colin 'Bert' Dredge says
he's the second oldest in the squad for Oxford, six years
behind Rose, who is 34. That's a dangerous age in that you can
have a bad season at 18 and 26 and no-one will worry, but woe
betide you if things go wrong at 34. They say you're finished.
I'm 27, by the way, and the fellow making his debut at
Cambridge is my brother, not my son.

Since I overslept this morning I only had a go on the ball
machine when Rose volunteered to put in the balls this afternoon. He was helpful, advising me to build up my strengths
rather than papering over my weaknesses. Shortly after that
the machine broke. Neither Rose, who is a gardener, nor I
understanding anything mechanical and so we returned to the
pavilion to watch the snooker on television.

We ended with a game we call handball, a mixture of
hockey and soccer in which we use our hands to pass a cricket
ball to each other. Rose says it's good for fielding and for team
spirit, which seems to ignore the fiery rows which erupt
minute by minute. Match abandoned at 4.30 and back home
for coffee at 5.

Friday 22 April

Hey, how about this? I came first in our cross-country run
today! Trainer Popplewell was running backwards and forwards, urging everyone on so he wasn't in the race, but the
rest of us were plodding around the 4½-mile course and
I won!

Hard to explain this change of form. Were I a horse, there
would be a stewards' enquiry. Maybe the looming black
clouds over St James' steeples forced me to step up the pace or
get soaked.

Our course ran from the ground back to my house and back to the ground. Offers of a tea-break at the halfway point were to no avail (though Gard and Marks may have had one to judge by the time they returned).

It's strange how many more hills there seem to be when you are running compared to when you are driving.

Anyway, it poured with rain all night and all day too, apart from most inconvenient bursts of sunshine which enabled us to start our marathon. Running is dreadful, isn't it? They had a marathon on TV the other day in which about 23,000 ran voluntarily! It looked spiritually uplifting as I sat at home in my armchair, but if it's six times as bad as what we did today, I'll be staying in my armchair next year, too.

So still only one bat on grass. Taunton is saturated and already next Monday's friendly at Bristol is in doubt. No-one really minds though, because there's nothing anyone can do except sit around, have a coffee and hope that it all dries up soon. We are in resigned mood. Week 3 is over, another 21 to go until the end of the season. What will it bring? No runs on the board yet.

Today 180 balls on the machine, the run, five cups of coffee, a photo call and this evening a pub 'do' for Skipper Rose's benefit fund.

Monday 25 April

It must, I suppose, have been the fault of the mountainous chicken cooked by Hallam Moseley at the weekend. I trundled in about sixth in our 2½-mile run.

Botham is back, appearing in the dressing room as we gasped for breath after our run. People were pleased to see him, he brightens things up. It's surprising how much time he and Richards spend at the County Ground. Even when they are not playing they stay in the dressing room, playing snooker, watching television or hanging about. They are at the ground much more than other players. Both are perhaps most comfortable in a dressing room where they are known and amongst sportsmen with whom they are at ease. Neither man cares a jot for business or files or organising things or reading or writing letters. That is not their world. Nor can they disappear into Taunton, it's too small a place for anonymity. Our dressing room is probably the only place apart from their homes where they are not threatened by anyone or anything. It's the only place no-one will be watching them, where their characters are taken for granted and not judged.

In the afternoon we had a final indoor net, though I preferred to used the ball machine. I gather Clive Rice, Gatting and Kallicharran rely upon these machines, too. It really is satisfying to do some repetitive practice again and to see drives going where they are supposed to go. Vic had a bash on it too but couldn't get the hang of it at all.

Tomorrow we're off to Oxford with a benefit game to play in the evening and then six days of first-class cricket against Oxford University and Nottinghamshire. We are utterly unprepared. I haven't batted with fieldsmen around me since January in Sydney and some of the fellows haven't played competitive cricket since September. For all the nets, for all the ball machines, nothing prepares you for standing with a bat in your hand, taking guard from an umpire with a blank scoreboard hovering over you and eleven fieldsmen out to dismiss you while it's still blank.

I hope I start well — it'll ease the strain and boost the confidence. I mean, I ought to do well but there's no guarantee whatever. Whenever I go in to bat I fear I'll score 0, though strangely this season I'm so short of match practice that I haven't formed any such gloomy attitude.

2

A Duck and a Swipe

Tuesday 26 April

A most enjoyable evening with Victor, chatting over a glass of wine and boeuf something or other at The Poor Student.

We talked at first about the importance of character in cricket, reflecting that the difference between the great and the very good appeared to be a final touch of commitment and extra spit in the core of personality. Compare Richards and Zaheer: both men have scored a large number of runs at the highest level and yet is there not something more substantial about Richards? Does he not impose his authority upon the game when its challenges are greatest? Richards and Botham – and other champions in sport – seem to have a deep conviction and an unshakeable confidence so they can succeed whatever difficulties present themselves. They do not have the tiny holes in their armour that worry other men. Or at least, that's what Marks and I concluded. It's not only ability that

separates these men: Colin Dredge's backhand sweep is every
bit as good as Botham's.

Later, as the pudding arrived, we discussed Somerset's
cricketing history, littered as it is with defeats plucked from
the jaws of victory, a litany of disaster disturbed only by an
odd triumph in improbable circumstances. Buccaneering folk
heroes – Gimblett, Sammy Woods, Wellard, Alley, Andrews
– were the hallmark of the club with the 1970s when
Cartwright and Close, men used to success, brought a new
professionalism. Following them, Rose and a group of home-
bred youngsters gathered, determined that the reputation of
the club as lovable losers must be changed.

Rose, Denning, Botham, Marks, Dredge, Roebuck were all
locals. Hallam Moseley had been here for years and Richards
quickly came to regard Somerset as a second home. We had a
young local team which grew up together. In 1978, Rose's first
year as Captain, we should have won two trophies but failed in
two never-to-be-forgotten days. We were shattered, as if all
our devoted efforts had proved only what everyone had been
saying all along: 'It's not in the nature of these West Country
fellows to win things. They can be magnificent on their day,
but they can't sustain it.' In 1979 we suffered the ignominy of
being thrown out of the Benson & Hedges Cup for declaring at
Worcester and, spurred on by this, fought back to reach a
dramatic final weekend for the second year running. This time
we broke through, won both the Gillette Cup and the John
Player League, and in so doing lost as much as we gained.

What we lost was the drive that an empty trophy shelf
brought. It has not been so easy to rediscover that pioneering
spirit. We won more cups in 1981 and 1982, but it was not so
satisfying. It is as if this group had climbed its mountain and
now could not find a new challenge. Other teams rely upon
hard professionalism to drive them along. Teams like
Leicestershire and Middlesex rigorously carry on day after
day, battling away. We seem to need some more distant sense
of purpose than professional competence. We need something
hot to chase.

So here we are, approaching 1983. Can we be as hungry as
our rivals? We shall see.

We had no trouble finding Oxford. Then Popplewell took
over as navigator. He said he had visited Oxford several times,

and I'd forgotten that I'd been born there. We could not find our hotel and spent 40 minutes cursing furiously. This is not a record. Last year in Derby we stopped to ask what turned out to be the same policeman three times for directions. The third time he said he'd arrest us if we asked him again. Our trouble was that, though we could nod sagely as instructions were given, no-one was ever listening. Marks is particularly weak in this area. When I asked him what the fellow had said, he replied that he hadn't a clue.

By the way, today's benefit game was cancelled. Our season starts tommorrow, after 1500 balls in the nets.

11.15 pm.   Torrential rain, thunder and lightning too. Why am I smiling? Why can I hear Somerset players singing in the corridors and opening windows to watch the rain fall? Why does it feel that the rain has delayed our being taken to the guillotine?

Wednesday 27 April

At breakfast there was a distinctly happy hysteria in the air, as if it were VE day. Men were not actually dancing over their eggs but they were beaming smiles and colleagues talked merrily to each other rather than gruffly acknowledging each other's existence. Even I joined the group for breakfast, a rare concession for the time of the day, a rare demonstration of solidarity.

It was pouring down, you see. For years I've thought this love of rain was an affectation, a parody of the few who genuinely vented their fury at every black cloud which refused to emply its bowels. I realise now my naivety. My own relief today was entirely genuine: I was happy that it was raining so hard. I reached this truth with reluctance. It is silly. Many of us have abandoned much to play cricket and here we are, wildly good-humoured because today's match will be abandoned.

Not wishing to tempt the fates, we arrived at the Parks at 9.30 and trudged out to inspect the pitch. Each man reported with a huge grin that it was like a swamp. We wouldn't play for a month, said Lloyds, not quite crestfallen. Immediately the rain routine began for the first time this season. Marks, Rose, Lloyds and Gard settled into a game of cards they'd play hour upon hour all over England. Others read the papers or went for a coffee or strolled about, wondering why it was so impossible to do anything useful on a wet cricket ground. I bought some boots in Oxford and wondered why everyone showing an iota of intelligence in the place appeared to be at least 50 and usually female.

After lunch the rain stopped and we had a long and valuable fielding practice, much our best since 1980. This was most encouraging, suggesting that we were serious in our intentions this year. Popplewell wore a collection of anoraks, shorts, bandages, hoods and running shoes as if we were going to some fancy dress party, and Marks couldn't resist appealing for every faint edge in the slip cordon. As I said, he spent his winter in Australia.

We stayed out for two hours before returning to our hotel, which is another of those assembly-line places where there are coffee-bags, television in the room and no-one cares who the hell you are.

I doubt if we'll start our game tomorrow. The pitch is really sodden.

Thursday 28 April

Morning.   Lord above, how little I feel like playing cricket today. My mind is in a stupor. I feel heavy and slow. It's a misty but dry morning so I suppose we might play later in the day but my mind is too dead for me to succeed. It's 8.30, I've had breakfast, I'm sitting in my room with my tapes and *Times* and for no reason whatever feeling gloomy.

11.30 am.   Needn't have worried. Pitch under water. Not much chance of playing today. Training, soccer and sitting around reading papers. There is some talk of golf, some talk of trying to arrange a game for tomorrow somewhere in the neighbourhood. Gooch scored 174 yesterday.

10.30 pm.   Returned home from evening in a pub. A pleasant afternoon wandering around the Parks. The trees are in lovely blossom but the Cherwell is filthy. I heard a cuckoo. The Parks are beautiful when you open up your eyes to them. After that I wandered around the bookshops of Oxford and bought six books which I'll never have time to read. Spent an hour or two reading the letters of F. Scott Fitzgerald.

We're supposed to be playing a 50-over friendly on a fresh strip tomorrow but it has been raining again so maybe we won't. A dry game in a wet land! Rose and I are secretly pleased at the abandonment of our first-class match here. Neither of us ever scores any runs at Oxford anyway and reckon that lesser rivals 'fill their boots' here.

Friday 29 April

v. Oxford University (friendly)
Out first ball! Can you believe it? A month of cross-country runs, 2000 balls on a bloody ball machine and I'm out first ball. It's outrageous.

My indignation has been slightly assuaged by beer, as it is 10 pm as I write and we've spent most of the evening driving towards Trent Bridge for tomorrow's game. We stopped in a pub along the way for steak and kidney pie. And anyway the whole thing was so preposterous that even I could see a faintly amusing side to it.

My first ball of the 1983 season was bowled by a gentleman of Oxford called Varey, who has established something of a reputation of a batsman but none at all as a bowler. It was a wet pitch and I'd planned to play back but, watching Varey's hiccoughing run-up, decided that I could safely push forward. As the ball came towards me I plunged out. The ball pitched on a length, rose amiably and touched my glove before lolloping to the wicket-keeper. I walked as soon as I felt the touch, not because I am a walker − a sanctimonious shower − but because there didn't seem much point in hanging around looking desperate. I gather the sound of leather on willow has pleased the poets. I can report that the sound of leather on glove is not remotely romantic.

Vic was in the dressing room as I returned so soon after setting out. No-one else was about, a moving tribute to my reputation as a dressing room curser. When I'm out the room is always silent. Whatever anyone says, it'll be the wrong thing. 'Bad luck' is worst of all, as I usually bark something about '——— luck has nothing to do with it.' Mind you, the dressing room used to empty as soon as Brian Close was out − any investigator would look at the half-drunk cups of coffee and think it a second *Marie Celeste*.

Vic realised that even I would be able to see the funny side of this one. He looked at me sheepishly as I flung down my bat. He could not help laughing as I exclaimed, 'Well, I'm buggered!' and to be honest, neither could I.

Several entertaining things happened today. Gary Palmer walked because the keeper said 'Well bowled' to one of the bowlers and Gary thought he must have been out. He was kindly informed of his mistake. Then Vic thought a ball had gone for four, so he poked down the pitch. It turned out that the ball had been retrieved inside the ropes and the fieldsmen removed the bails with Vic still prodding down the pitch. That appeal was withdrawn too, much to my disappointment because it would have been a splendid dismissal. Also I did catch a couple of sharp ones in the slips, which cheered me up, and Vic did drop an easy one and split his trousers in the process which cheered me even more.

I spent my not inconsiderable amount of spare time reading more of Scott Fitzgerald's letters on a bench under a tree in the Parks. I mention this because I came across the following which struck a chord: '. . . the thing that lies behind all great careers from Shakespeare's to Abraham Lincoln's and as far back as there are books to read — the sense that life is essentially a cheat and its conditions are those of defeat and that the redeeming things are not "happiness and pleasure" but the deeper satisfaction that comes out of the struggle.'

Oxford U. 121 for 8, Somerset 92 for 6

Saturday 30 April

v. Nottinghamshire at Nottingham (1st day)
It's 10.40 pm as I write this, having returned from an Italian restaurant in Nottingham where five of us enjoyed lasagne, chicken and carafes of wine. Now they've gone to play snooker and I'm in my room half watching 'Match of the Day'.

We had our first taste of county cricket today on a wet pitch at Trent Bridge. A thunderstorm had defeated the covers so parts of the wicket were soaked. Luckily we won the toss and they had to bat.

I'd forgotten how good county cricket can be and how competitive it is at its best. It was a real battle between bat and ball, an aggressive duel. Their batsmen hit the ball hard and, though we bowled some rubbish, we also bowled some deliveries that took a lot of playing. Their batsmen struck me as healthily robust. It was most enjoyable in a way, a reminder that I'd have to fight to hold my head up in this company. Sometimes in the winter I forget just how competitive, how tough this professional cricket is, how unrelenting it can be if you're soft in the head. Every April I remember and value the advice given to me years ago by Brian Close. He said, 'Always work in the winter, lad, or your mind'll get lazy.' For Close, a lazy mind was the greatest enemy a cricketer could have.

Before the game I was incredibly nervous. It was ridiculous to be so tense on such a sunlit day at such a lovely ground. Yet I was almost sick with worry. I had a headache before the toss, I was edgy with trying to work out how to bat against Hadley on a flyer. Really, it's only cricket, it's stupid to fret so much.

As it turned out we were in the field without a chance of batting and there was nothing to worry about. I spent the afternoon in the slips, chatting to Botham and Marks, mostly about what sort of egg it was best to have for breakfast. Of course we did concentrate hard when the bowler was bowling, but cricket is played 6½ hours a day for 105 days out of 125 and it's vital to drift away between balls and between days.

This morning, as a few more hours slumbered by, I read my book. All was quiet until Botham introduced a game of cards involving racing and gambling. He offered odds on which suit would have eight cards down first. There were odds because seven cards had already been withdrawn and could be seen. The races were very exciting, honestly! I was his clerk, calling the odds and taking the bets. Botham was as loud as ever, informing the umpires that it was silly to play on a wet pitch and expecting everyone to join in the noisy fun of the card races.

I saw Ian a few times in Australia during the winter. He tried terribly hard — he gives to his cricket immense lumps of his personality — but his spirit was somehow dulled by the experience. I read something Peter Ustinov said to Bjorn Borg the other day and it brought Botham to mind: 'You know how to get your effect; it's second nature to you. Then suddenly you reach a point, either you're tired or you've been working too hard, when you have to analyse how you did it. You have to rediscover that something spontaneous, to try to imitate yourself, to try to regain it by doing it consciously, and that ruins everything.'

Borg retired at 26, though Lord alone knows how he'll ever find anything as exciting in the rest of his life to match the peak of his tennis career. Botham is 27, he has endured seven years' battering to body and spirit. He plays 70 days' international cricket a year, much more than they were expected to play in olden days. What's more, like Borg, Botham's whole life is held up for examination. He is public property. I hope we will not lose our most precious possession through expecting too much of him. Mind you, I wonder if Botham will be able to find anything in his later years to replace the heady excitement of his life now.

Notts 181 for 6

Sunday 1 May

The rain started at 2 am this morning and it hasn't stopped yet. Trent Bridge is smothered with puddles. We'll not play tomorrow. And so I enter May without having scored a run yet. So far I've been paid about £1200 this season. I caught two catches at Oxford and didn't bowl, which means I'm on about £600 a catch — rather more, I think, than baseball players.

We had an excellent morning spent playing Botham's game of horse races with new rules developed by Roebuck. We put two jokers in the pack and announced that every time a joker came out, the horses in the lead fell. With any luck we could cut out two or three joint leaders when the joker emerged, which meant that anyone backing those suits lost. This caused much wild excitement and no little profit. Actually the room was filled with hysterical shouts as men roared 'Come on, spades', 'Get on, my boy', 'What the hell's clubs' jockey doing?', 'Get the whip out, man!' and so on. It really is a tremendous game which went on for two hours with Botham winning £25 and everyone extremely excited by the host of close finishes. It was emotional, you know, when you were on spades to win and they led all the way, only to be wiped out at the final fence by the appearance of the joker. All those roars, all those hoarse cheers to waste.

Back to the hotel after lunch to watch the world snooker

final on television. I'm off to see *Tootsie* this evening. There really isn't much to do in our small musty rooms except read and write.

Monday 2 May

Waterlogged ground. Left Nottingham at 9.30 to drive home. It's been a lovely week. I still haven't scored my first run of the season.

The cherry blossom is out in my garden. I've no food in the house and all the shops are closed, it's a Bank Holiday apparently. So I went to the ground and found almost everyone in our dressing room playing snooker and eating sausages and eggs.

Tuesday 3 May

Went into the ground for a go on the ball machine but our indoor school was full of tables and chairs for sponsor's lunches for tomorrow's home game. Had a bat on the artificial pitch. I was woeful. I suppose I haven't had a bat for a week and all that practice seems years ago. The pitch looks fine for tomorrow's match. I'll have to put my head down and see if I can stay in long enough to get some sort of system working, some sort of pattern to my technique.

I hope the rain stops, honestly I do.

Wednesday 4 May

v. Worcestershire at Taunton (1st day)
81. I scored 81 today. Not bad eh? I was out for 0 and 1 in our first game last year, and I was hit on the jaw.

I hit a six too, my first one in Championship cricket for years. I think it's partly my higher backlift and partly this Duncan Fearnley bat, which seems to hit the ball further than any bat I've ever had before. Last year, when I hit a six in a John Player League game, a spectator called out, 'Good Lord, I've seen it all now.'

I was out bowled, or rather played on, trying to hit the ball off the back foot past point. Do you remember that I wasn't ever going to play that shot? Jeremy Lloyds said that he thought at first I was going for a hook and since that was never my intention I must have positioned myself abysmally for the stroke. This is a technical weakness. It's a shot I play with a cross-bat and it's no wonder I'm out to it so often.

Strangely, I can recall what I was thinking as Pridgeon ran in to bowl that ball. It seemed to me that there was nothing mental or physical preventing me scoring a century and I was reflecting how nice it would be and how it would surprise and cheer my friends in Australia. And so I was out. Of course, it's perfectly possible I was thinking other distracting things for other balls and survived.

It's funny how when you bat, your mind forms a theme to help it concentrate. Some people count the balls of the over, others curse themselves and goad themselves to concentrate. Others simply study the ball in the bowler's hand as he runs in. My theme today was to do my job well. I kept saying to myself 'Do your job.' It was a pity to fall short of 100. I have a terrible record of scoring centuries, with only five in my career. No point in worrying about it, though, it would only make matters worse. It was a pleasure to hit some good straight drives and even one or two off-drives, though a few of these still ended up at long leg. My off-side play remains weak.

After I was out, I strolled round town, paid my mortgage and bought a plug for my razor. A worker on a building site hailed me and asked after the score. I replied, '150 for 2', and he asked if I fancied swopping jobs. I said no, but that he was to ask me again when we were playing against Holding.

Finally, Viv Richards returned today. He strolled into the dressing room at lunchtime, fresh off his plane. The Antigua Test finished only last night. Wearing a brown leather cap and brown leather jacket, he was as impeccable as ever and immediately added laughter to our company. He greeted everyone warmly, teased a few and cracked some jokes. You could tell he was pleased to be back and his bubbling, emotional personality gave everyone a lift. Not that anyone takes him lightly. I can remember the day in 1978, after our defeats in September, when he went into the bathroom and in his despair smashed his bat to pieces. You don't meddle with people like that.

Somerset 325 for 7 dec.

Thursday 5 May

v. Worcestershire at Taunton (2nd day)

Will it ever stop? The rain is tumbling down as it had threatened to all day. We played between the showers and in the most treacherous conditions. At one stage Botham tucked his trousers into his socks like a cyclist. In the end a muddy outfield, leaden skies and a ball like a bar of soap defeated us all. We played just long enough for me to drop a catch.

There were a few people dotted around the ground, ones and twos here and there. I suppose most of them look forward all winter to their season's cricket. Being English, none of them talked to each other and none of them budged an inch in the heaviest shower. They just sat there in raincoats with flasks of coffee, reading their *Telegraph* or their *Times*, patiently waiting for the heavens to relent. We must be a stoical lot to be able to sit in misery on rickety benches and all to see me drop Phil Neale at third slip off Colin Dredge.

What time we had in the field was spent chatting to Botham and Marks in the slips. Marks split another pair of trousers and Botham caught a catch with astonishing brilliance. My catch was easy, by the way. It landed in my hands but immediately jumped out again. My hands must be too hard. Why I am in the slips I cannot say (I never catch anything), unless it's because I'm now a senior player and a Cambridge graduate and all educated people seem to field in the slips. Both Marks and I prefer to lounge at long leg, chewing the grass.

I avoided the papers today as much I could. They're bound to use some adjectives to describe my innings (except *The Times* – Alan Gibson writes for them and his train is usually late and so he misses my knock) and I don't want anyone else's judgements disturbing my own analysis. If they'd said I was studious I'd probably go and try to be studious tomorrow, hoping for a second good score. Their description would become my prescription, a solution in the never-ending search for a successful formula which might disrupt the fresh spirit that I must bring to each and every innings.

This idea of finding a successful formula sustains cricketers like the belief in Eldorado sustained explorers. It's something you cling to when times are hard. You find it expressed not only in superstition but in lifestyle, too. Last year I found myself, ridiculously, wearing a dirty old sweater, long-sleeved shirt and track-suit bottoms because that was what I wore in scoring my first fifty of the season. I even wore that jumper in the Benson & Hedges final. Later, when form deserted — and you'll scarcely believe this of a Cambridge graduate — I read *The Inner Game* and tried to repeat its formula (avoid tension, regard your body as an object to be trained, look at the ball as an interesting object, above all 'let it happen') and later I tried Ginsing tea every morning because Gavaskar and Richards take it. As a friend observed, 'You haven't scored any runs since you took that funny tea, have you?' Great heavens above, I even have a lucky loo in the changing room.

It's absurd, I know. Yesterday I wore a long-sleeved shirt and a sleeveless jumper. If it's cold tomorrow I'm damned well going to wear a long-sleeved jumper.

Our trainer, Dennis Waight, whom we call 'Bilko' after his favourite TV character, returned today. Bilko takes us on a fifteen-minute stretch before play every day, the idea being to prevent pulled or strained muscles. He also slaps ice on injured bits. But his value is much more subtle than this. He is a hard, pugnacious Australian who treats everyone the same; he's just as likely to call Botham a billy-goat or a tart as he is a younger player. I've never seen him lose his temper, and his rough humour relieves our downcast moments. He runs six miles every day. In the evening of every away trip he's permanently installed in the bar, gin and tonic in hand, ready to talk entertainingly with whoever presents themselves. If you are lucky, Bilko will recall his days as a traveller round the world. Once he found himself in Mexico, living on 50 cents a day. He stayed in a poor house with some peasants who gave him a hearty breakfast of bacon and sausages every morning, after which he'd repair to the stone lavatory. He never could work out where the debris went until he saw one of the pigs enter the gents just after he'd left. He gave up breakfast after that.

Somerset 325 for 7 dec., Worcs 78 for 1

Friday 6 May
v. Worcestershire at Taunton (3rd day)
This evening at the end of the game, Richards batted in the nets, facing our coach, Peter Robinson, and Gary Palmer.

Every Somerset player lingered in the dressing room, watching him through the windows, a tribute rarely paid to any cricketer. He appeared to be in his most disdainful mood, defending only a few balls and smashing the rest where he wanted.

Richards' technique is astonishing. Against even the fastest bowlers he steps forward, waiting to drive. If the ball is short he pulls it from in front of his face with a panache that says, 'You see? You cannot drive me back. You cannot bowl short to Smoky.' In his World Series days he used to bait Pascoe into bowling shorter and shorter, calling down the pitch after each bumper, 'Butter, Lennie, butter,' and later 'Marmalade, Lennie, marmalade' to provoke more short stuff.

Unless the ball is very wide, Viv will straight-drive, or whip to leg with a late roll of the wrists. Even in that prodigious leg stroke, the bat is staring straight down the pitch at the umpire until the moment of contact. When he means business, that bat is very, very wide, never angling to off or to leg. He often straight-drives from a foot outside off stump. Perhaps that straight bat is why Richards has, I think, the best defence I've ever seen.

If Richards were content to rely upon his studied defence he'd hardly fail. But, of course, that isn't his notion of batting. He wants to dominate, to destroy and, in seeking to show his mastery, sometimes he brings about his own downfall as he tries to hit balls that deserve no such treatment. And inevitably after all these years at the top, sometimes he fails because the game fails to stir him. He's not much use unless he is stirred, he dislikes doing anything, let alone batting, in a casual way. He succeeds most when he is aroused, a lion on the rampage.

Garner arrived, too, popping in to say hello in his deep Bajan voice. His arrival, Bilko's and Viv Richards' complete the team.

Today's cricket is best forgotten. Vic dropped two more catches, including one off his own bowling. This was a skier and upon reflection I might have had a go at it myself. Anyway, Vic wobbled under it, called 'Mine' none too enthusiastically and dumped it on the ground.

This wasn't the best dropped catch I've seen. There is nothing in cricket more calculated to raise a laugh than the sight of some determined and serious man under a spiralling catch. Last season at the Oval, Rose and I were the only out-fielders when Clarke lashed a ball high into the clouds. Rose bellowed 'Mine', an unnecessary precaution since I'd already decided to maintain a stout silence. He proceeded to circle under the ball like a Red Indian circling a wagon train. He stepped first this way and then that, trying to calculate the ball's flight. As it fell to earth he flung himself through the air and still didn't manage to interrupt its downward path as he fell to the ground with a crash. He, alone amongst us, did not entirely recognise the hilarity of those moments.

Tomorrow we meet Sussex in our first Benson & Hedges game. We are in an extremely tough group – Sussex, Hampshire and Essex – and we'll do well to survive. But everyone is eager and I wouldn't put it beyond us this season. So far I've had only one innings out of six. Four more await me before the end of May.

Somerset 325 for 7 dec., Worcs 253 for 7

Saturday 7 May

B & H v. Sussex at Taunton (1st day)

I was out to a dreadful swipe today. We started well after being put in to bat (although both Barclay and Rose thought they'd won the toss, Rose backed down because he had cotton-wool in his ears, but he strode into our dressing room to say, 'I'm ——— sure he said heads'). Then they brought on their left-arm spinner, Waller. With unswerving devotion to my new-found principles, I whacked his first ball over his head for four. Barclay set the field back and an over passed. I faced Waller again and this time Barclay brought the field in. I tried to wallop one over deep mid-wicket, turned the face of the bat, lent back, lifted my head and skied the ball to point.

What made this dismissal even more of a cock-up was that Barclay had only brought the field in because he'd thought it was Roebuck, not Lloyds, who was on 49!

Home at 8.30 to round off a 12-hour day and then immediately off to my local with John Barclay. John is a fellow who strains and stresses all day and needs to unwind away from his team in the evening. Despite his Etonian accent and aristocratic façade, he is a tough, rigorous professional. His approach to cricket is not what his manner or background suggest, any more than is mine.

'Big Bird' Garner, by the way, said today that he was 'done swipin' '. We shall see. We are in a strong position in this Benson & Hedges game which will be continued on Monday after the rains of today. Tomorrow we have a John Player League game against Sussex.

Somerset 251 for 7 (55 overs)

Sunday 8 May

JPL v. Sussex at Taunton

Morning. Popped into Joel's for a coffee. Hallam was cooking something for this evening. He says he has been practising his hooking. Joel barked about, mixing hilarious anecdote with outrage at this and that. Waving his arms about, he explained that he was serious about his batting this year. West Indians use this word 'serious' to express a courageous commitment (the Gurkhas are 'serious'). Joel said that no-one had been able to dismiss him in this winter's Tests (I checked! J. Garner 4 innings, 4 not-outs, 24 runs). He said he would have scored more runs if his partners hadn't felt the need to hit out as soon as he came in. I rather suspect that the sight of Joel lumbering out with his matchstick bat and huge grin has that effect on most partners. Anyway, Holding had 'petted a lash' at Shastri and another time had 'swiped at Dev', leaving Garner high and dry.

When he is serious, Joel is utterly convincing. He described his experiences on a ball machine in Adelaide (the balls seemed to hit him more than he hit them) and added that Inverarity — 'a serious man, a 40-year old man who stands behind the ball when the others run' — had given him some lessons. No longer, he affirmed, did he plunge forward as if there were a five-foot crevice in front of the crease. He was going to score more runs.

Hallam didn't really agree. He said Joel couldn't really resist spinners. 'As soon as one floats into the sky, the eyes catch alight', and mighty was the swing. Joel said no, he'd resisted Venkat all winter and repeated that he was 'done swipin' '.

Night. Dined on Hallam's chicken at Joel's place, listening to more stories of Big Bird's days in Barbados. He told of a fellow who played for his club who had only four fingers and liked to gamble. Once he laid $300 that Joel could bowl out a rival team in an afternoon. He said, 'I ain't talkin' 'bout it, no way, here's the money.' It had taken Joel two hours to dismiss G. A. Greenidge, but he found an edge in the end and the rest ran.

Before our game today, an egg-sized lump appeared on my shin. I've no idea what caused it. Joel said it was cancer, but then last year when Viv had a cough he diagnosed TB. Bilko strapped me up and shoved me on the field, forgetting to strap my ankle which is sore too, so that I limped through my innings except when I had to run a quick one. As a matter of fact I'm a bit of a hypochondriac.

We won, by the way, scoring 213 (Richards 96, Roebuck 50). I have a habit of being out for 50. Either I relax or I try to accelerate too suddenly. Have to sort it out. Musn't do it again.

The *Sunday Times* carried an article today about the fellows who share our dressing room. It said they were nannies to the players. We have some back-room men; Pete McCombe helps Viv, Andy Withers helps Ian, and Chris Greenslade helps Joel. All nip in and out of our dressing room from time to time. Cricketers need support and inspiration. Wasn't it Bob Paisley who said his main job was to take the pressure off his players? That's what Pete, Andy and Chris do. They are not so much a part of the apparatus of superstardom, not so much one of the attachments of fame, as friends who lend a hand and offer encouragement when times are hard. Their contributions range from emotional punch-bags to chefs.

Somerset 213 for 5, Sussex 124

Monday 9 May

B & H v. Sussex at Taunton (2nd day)
An easy victory on a bitter cold day. Absolutely frozen in the field.

Vic caught a catch today.

Botham arrived this morning and sent someone to fetch a coffee and a pork pie. He has no fridge in his house. Viv said, 'Oh my, a man who has done so much for England, the best all-rounder in the world, comes to the ground in the morning for a pork pie to break his fast.'

In the evening I went off to Pete McCombe's to round off a jovial day. Peter is Viv's man, a roly-poly Scotsman who took care of Viv when he first arrived unknown in Taunton in 1974. Viv has never forgotten that and still Pete drives Richards everywhere, acting as his friend and advisor. They make a strange pair: Viv ever immaculate and polite, McCombe of Falstaffian grandeur with his pot belly and rough expressions. Friends call him the working man's mayor. He knows everyone in Taunton.

Tonight 'Falstaff' talked about his days with the parachutists in National Service. He'd joined in 1952 so that he could see the world, only to spend his entire National Service in Swindon. He said he spent 2½ of his four years in the glass-house and that at his court martial the sergeant had warned the court not to be misled by his angelic face, his blue eyes or his Scottish accent as 'This man's a nutter.'

Somerset 251 for 7, Sussex 192

Wednesday 11 May

v. Worcestershire at Worcester (1st day)

Porridge at the hotel, the first of the season. It's another of those hotels who book you in and sift you through without ever discovering your name, but this is more than made up by the choice of porridge on the breakfast menu.

After breakfast Marks and I wandered around Worcester Cathedral. We saw Elgar's grave and the Magna Carta and some lovely intimate chapels. Last time Vic and I visited a cathedral of a morning was in Salisbury. That day I scored 131 not out and Vic a duck. I think it was I who suggested our tour this morning.

After that auspicious start it ought to have been a good day. It was not. It was cold enough for most of us to sport long johns and I misfielded three times. We didn't apply ourselves today. It's a hard slog in the Championship, day after day after day. It's difficult to be enthusiastic all the time, especially when it's cold and the pitch is slow. That is, of course, why the Championship is the ultimate test of a team.

I don't like Worcester. They say it's a pretty ground but I

find the atmosphere unsympathetic. All the businessmen group in the sponsor's room with their backs to the cricket even when Richards and Botham are on the field, while the players lunch in the dressing room surrounded by wet towels, sweaty shirts and jockstraps. This puts the cricketers firmly in their place. I don't think a few fir trees and a distant cathedral can make up for this drab atmosphere. Imagine having to eat lunch in a cramped wet dressing room.

I do like the old potato wagon behind the Ladies' pavilion, though even that is broken.

This evening Vic and I searched for our favourite Greek restaurant. We've dined there every trip for eight years. We only went there to cheer up the owner and we never found anyone else there. The food was mediocre, the service desultory and the dining room shabby. What aroused our sympathy was the almost aristocratic refusal of the owner to try to attract custom. To our dismay we found the restaurant boarded up, bankrupt and long gone. So we went across the road to enjoy a meal in a far superior restaurant.

We have one more Championship game in May. I'll have batted four times at the most by the end of the month. Didn't people use to score 1000 runs before May turned to June?

Worcs 329 for 9

Thursday 12 May

v. Worcestershire at Worcester (2nd day)
3.45. It's pouring down. We're 66 for 0, Lloyds 26, Roebuck 27, and rain has stopped play. I batted dreadfully, frantically jabbing about. I've lost my off stump. That's the worst thing that can happen. If you don't know which balls are on the stumps and which balls aren't, you end up fiddling at everything.

Another habit has emerged. It appears I'm hooking this year. I haven't hooked for years, ever since the bravado of it seemed less important than the dismissals. It only encourages the quicker bowlers to bang them down again and again, their pride wounded. I've been hit on the head four times already (Roberts 2, Le Roux 1, Hacker 1) and don't plan any more if I can help it. Yet here we are, hooking as bold as can be. It's not planned nor even wanted, it's just happening. Today Warner banged one down and before I could think better of it I had whacked it through mid-wicket to the fence. Must stop doing that somehow. It isn't a good business shot for me.

I hit the left-arm spinner back over his head for a couple of fours in one over, though. That resolution is holding firm. They took him off.

We could have played earlier in the day. There was no need to start as late as ten past one. These things depend upon the umpires. There are some who think it is the greatest fun to be in the middle, getting on with the game. Others take a different view, arguing that there are better things in life. Here we have two of the latter persuasion. One returned from an inspection to exclaim that the ground staff were doing 'more harm than good with that squidgy thing' but that no-one was to tell them; he added jovially that it was 'even wetter than yesterday'. When we did play, a 'big black 'un' approached and I whispered that if they offered us the light, we could all rush off before the storm broke. It'd be silly, I explained, to stay on until the rain began to fall; it'd be like being killed on Armistice Day. No more play.

Worcs 329 for 9, Somerset 66 for 0

Friday 13 May

v. Worcestershire at Worcester (3rd day)

Read the papers. *The Guardian* says I played and missed all the time. *The Times* says I smashed them all over the place and gives me a headline: 'Roebuck's relish' (it was a slow news day). My relish was to play bridge.

Today I started batting at 1.40 pm on 27 and returned to the pavilion at five past two, bowled for 28. I'd even left my steak and kidney pie uneaten. Now it's 3.30 and I'm hungry. This evening we face a long cross-country journey to Chelmsford.

God, how I hate getting out. I poked around again. Edged in a single somewhere and then had my off stump knocked back. It was a good ball, at least I think it was. I say it left me and kept low. My partner, Richards, says it kept low and nipped back. It was probably straight.

Now the spinners are on and the lower-order men are helping themselves like hungry men at a buffet. What a waste of runs! It's ironic that figures, which used to be an interesting by-product of the game, now dominate a cricketer's thoughts. It's as if we are models who must have good figures if our services are to be used. We're judged in cold statistics each September and if we can't provide evidence of our worth, we'll be sacked.

10.45 pm.   At last our harrowing trip to Chelmsford is over. It was an infuriating journey behind endless Uncle Joes and Aunt Ediths off to see their confounded nephews and nieces. The journey took us five hours, all spent in my car except for gammon and chips in a pub. Tomorrow night it's off to Nottingham and then perhaps back to Chelmsford if necessary before finally ending our tour in Taunton.

When I was young I used to follow Somerset's scores. One day they'd be in Eastbourne and the next in Leeds. It never occurred to me that they had to sit in a car for four hours in between.

Our room is steamy and hot and to be frank, life's been better! Goodbye to Friday the 13th.

Worcs 329 for 9, Somerset 301 for 5

3

Up and Down, In and Out

Saturday 14 May

B & H v. Essex at Chelmsford
4.45 pm.   Tea-time at Chelmsford. We are 85 for 4 and chasing
Essex's 225. They were 115 for 6 at lunch but we were hopeless
after that. They had a lot of luck. I asked Rose if the lbw rule
had been scrapped for the day.

Can we win? Richards is still in but we're in trouble. They
say this is our jinx ground, but how can that be so? It's only a
field with some stumps in the middle, so how can it be jinxed?
We rarely win here, though, that's true. I never understand this
home advantage thing in cricket. But today Richards said that
whenever he comes to Chelmsford, it's as if he can't time the
ball any more and I found the same trouble, which isn't quite as

unusual. Maybe the wickets are slightly different to the ones we are used to on our own ground.

I was run out by two yards. I'd just hit Stuart Turner for a straight six as well. Viv called me for an impossible single and Turner threw down the stumps with me only just entering the final furlong.

That was an hour ago. I muttered considerably on the way back to the pavilion and hurled the bat into my bag. I've recovered now and yet something is worrying me beyond that initial anger.

Didn't I feel a sense of release when I saw the stumps broken? Wasn't I relieved the team's fortunes had passed on to the shoulders of someone else without any fault on my part? I wonder if the most courageous soldier secretly hopes for an honourable injury that preserves self-esteem and enables withdrawal from danger without loss of respect.

It's hard to explain that feeling. It's as if you tense yourself not to let your team-mates down and yet all the time there is the fear of cocking things up by scoring too slowly. A dismissal entirely someone else's fault saves you from that fraught problem.

There's no point in adding to Viv's sorrow by ignoring him. We chatted amiably as soon as he came in for tea and he's sitting next to me as I write. Last time he ran me out, he tried so hard to redeem himself that he strangled all his shots and lost his wicket. Today he's our last hope of saving the game. He's trying quite hard enough already.

Nottingham, 10.30 pm. Lost by 50 runs. Three idiotic run-outs, Botham out to a back-handed sweep. Essex had a concerted appeal every time Richards and Botham were hit on the pad. I wonder if they practise that.

But our defeat was our own fault. We batted like pilots who couldn't resist the odd Kamikaze mission.

It was a surprisingly cheerful trip up to Nottingham. We stopped in a lovely old coaching pub halfway between London and York and listened to a strange radio play in the car. Vic travelled with me. He says all his shots end up at gully and I said all mine end up at square leg and we laughed at our various absurdities before turning in.

Essex 225 for 8, Somerset 172

Sunday 15 May

JPL v. Nottinghamshire at Nottingham

Arrived home from Nottingham at 9.30 pm and ordered a Chinese take-away. It has been a good day. For no detectable reason at all, my dented confidence returned. I could feel it even before the game. My body felt fluent and my strokes were in tune. In the middle I hit my first two balls for four. I've never done that before, never.

I can tell when I'm in form. I don't search for runs as starving mice search for crumbs. I don't try to hit the ball too hard nor decide before it's bowled where it's going to go. Nor do I try to correct weaknesses as I bat. In form I simply bat in my own way, not giving a damn whether it's classical or entertaining and not trying to imitate other batsmen. If my technique is not working I do ridiculous things like trying to copy Richards or Zaheer. It never works — how could it? In form I know that my best way of scoring runs is to be myself, and I have the confidence to believe that this will be good enough.

I scored 46 in 57 balls. It didn't feel as if I was batting against my body. It didn't feel as if my bat had a life of its own. Standing at the crease felt a natural thing, not some artistic pose held to please some modern sculptor.

When I was out, Richards was joined by Botham, who had taken a terrible pasting from the papers after his dismissal yesterday. As we crossed I nearly said, 'Good luck, but for Pete's sake don't try that back-handed sweep' but thought I'd better not. Botham broke his duck inevitably with that stroke and proceeded to pound 85 in 13 overs, adding 138 in that time with Richards. There wasn't much Nottinghamshire could do; these two seemed able to hit leg-side yorkers from Hadlee over third man if they chose. They were helped by Hemmings bowling faster and flatter when he was attacked. Marks doesn't do that. He bowls more slowly if anything, forcing the batsmen to hit straight.

What a contrast in two days. Nottinghamshire were well behind the run-rate when rain prevented further play.

Somerset 279 for 3, Nottinghamshire 32 for 1 (11 overs)

Monday 16 May

No match. Torrential rain all day.

Tuesday 17 May

B & H v. Hampshire at Taunton (1st day)

Oh Lord! In what's supposed to be a vital game, two hours of play, starting at 3.30 on a wet outfield. If we lose, we're out of the competition. Returned home with Vic this morning to listen to some records, then lunch and sitting around for two hours.

The delays dented the atmosphere and the cold weather and turbulent winds brought a prosaic mood to this important day. We did well, though, taking three wickets for 78 runs in 33 overs.

Everyone was miserable. There was a fraught atmosphere this morning. I was in a filthy mood too, for no particular reason except feeling this tension and disappointment with the dreadful weather. We'd come ready for a big game and had to sit around, gradually deflating.

Greenidge is playing for Hampshire, his first game back after the terrible death of his daughter which moved and saddened everyone so much. He sat in our dressing room chatting to Viv and Joel most of the morning, obviously deeply upset, but he courageously scored 35 not out in their innings.

It has been a grumbling, glum day.

Hants 78 for 3 (33 overs)

Wednesday 18 May

B & H v. Hampshire at Taunton (2nd day)

We suffered an absolutely shattering defeat. The game finished only 30 minutes ago. We had to score 139 in 55 overs and failed. We cracked under pressure. I looked around the dressing room and thought, 'You mean this lot can't score 139?'

I left immediately after the game. There were a lot of grim faces. Viv had popped home on an errand. When he left we were 65 for 2; when he returned we were 94 for 8. He whispered to me, 'How did this happen, tell me, how did this happen?' There was no possible answer except to say that we left it all to each other.

I scored 21, which was top score. I was out caught at slip, trying to drive Jesty. Maybe I'd lost a little concentration, it's hard to say. When you're chasing a small total, it seems as if you could just hit a few fours and win the game easily. But Jesty is one of those bowlers who entices you to play drives and then swings one a bit wide and you go after it. If I'd been able to keep practising on the ball machine, I'm sure I'd have played the drive safely.

Our collapse was feeble. We were soft-headed, losing the game in a half-hour when we lost concentration individually and collectively. I could have stayed in longer, and so could nearly everyone else. Quite simply we needed to be much more tenacious. We forgot that you have to fight very hard from the first ball to the last if you mean to win.

And so we have lost our chance in the Benson & Hedges competition in most depressing circumstances. We left it all to each other. We've never been much good at qualifying games — perhaps the flavour of a Lord's final was too distant for us today.

Hants 138, Somerset 114

Thursday 19 May

Why did we lose yesterday? Outsiders say they can sense a certain unease at the club, as if success were sitting uncomfortably with us. Perhaps it is. Some clubs have a long history of Championship and cup successes. It took us over 100 years to win anything. In five years we have achieved so much — not just trophies, but a new pavilion, a cricket shop, huge crowds, school coaching schemes, executive boxes, bowling machines, all-weather nets and our very own trainer. When Marks, Botham, Richards and I joined Somerset, we used to change in a little stone hut behind the old pavilion, and our ground was a dingy, ramshackle place of which it was hard to be proud. We have advanced far in a few years; we are rather like a newly independent state which has created a democracy but is not quite sure how to live with it.

Nor is it surprising that the team has lost a little of its fire. It's not only that we've achieved our most effective ambition — of bringing success to the county and its deserving supporters — but since 1978 many of us have married, bought houses, started families and developed alternative careers. It all seems to matter less.

Saturday 21 May

B & H v. Minor Counties at Slough

Up to Slough. (Mr Justice Melford Stevenson once said to a convict, 'I see you come from Slough. It's a horrible place. You can go back there.') Travelled with a young pro who talked about his love life most of the way in a breezy manner, so much so that I found myself going up the M5 when I should have been going along the M4. He sought my advice in unravelling his knots but I told him that cricket pros should only say things like 'Keep your left elbow up, lad' to each other.

Arrived at ground at 9.45 from Windsor Hotel. Game abandoned at 9.55. Probably won't play on Monday either. Drove to London to a lovely antique hotel in Swiss Cottage run by ladies from the camps. The rooms here have chairs and tables and you feel at home. They have touches of comfort that are beyond the merely necessary. Also the girls are friendly and bright and not too efficient (nor is the lift). You feel more like a human being in these places rather than some remote star banished from contact with real people. It was here that Brian Rose had one of his best moments. When a German was being incredibly rude at breakfast, pompously berating the waitresses for their supposed inefficiency, Rose stood up and thundered across the room to the ladies that they were to ignore the rude man, who should hold his peace. We were all astonished and impressed by Rose's outburst.

From the hotel I caught an underground train to the West End. Lunch in a café and then a stroll round Trafalgar Square, a burst of freedom, a place to roam where people and pigeons know nothing of cricket. Popped into the National Gallery because it happened to be there and at 2.30 off to the first of three plays I saw today. First *Pirates of Penzance* in Drury Lane — marvellous; are professional actors really as joyous as that or do they all hate each other? Next *The Real Thing* in which Tom Stoppard showed to a Scottish revolutionary that just as a lump of wood isn't necessarily a good cricket bat, so a string of words isn't necessarily good writing. Finally, after a pizza, to *Another Country* at Queens. I didn't escape from cricket in this play, either. Austin Mitchell used a school game as the background for his penultimate scene. His team included a Marxist, a homosexual, a liberal, a sadist and, although we didn't see the other seven, I expect there was a leg-spinner too.

Finally, wearily back to the hotel to sleep. By the way, I bumped into Popplewell and Vic Marks' wife in *The Real Thing*. I think the rest watched the FA Cup Final.

Sunday 22 May

JPL v. Surrey at the Oval

I haven't slept well lately. Last night my room-mate had a violent cough which erupted through the small hours and prevented sleep, but before that the reason was a certain unease in our group. One of the hardest things in cricket is to sleep, dine, drink, play and travel with the same fellows, always sharing the same dressing room and always relying on each other on the field. We have not chosen each other as friends, yet we are thrown together, living in each other's pockets for six months. It is a fine balance to strike, to cast aside your personal prejudices and slip into a cohesive team without losing your individuality. Inevitably there are rows which are mostly unspoken, suppressed for the sake of that wobbling thing, team spirit.

At the moment, probably because we're doing badly, our conflicting characters are more to the fore than usual. If a fellow is scoring lots of runs or taking lots of wickets, colleagues very quickly forgive his quirks. But in a team which is struggling, these tensions tend to edge nearer to the surface. What's more, most of this group have very strong characters: if they had not, they would not survive in cricket at all. And this of course sharpens the conflict.

And so, at the moment, my nerves are too tight to admit easy sleep.

It does not help that a county cricket team, especially away from home, leads such a removed life: from posh hotel to ground and back to posh hotel, with breakfasts and other meals served to order. This encourages us to regard ourselves as stars, as something extraordinary. And yet what are we except men who ply a trade, just as blacksmiths and watchmakers do? Most of us come from humble backgrounds − Denning's dad is a butcher, Marks' is a farmer, Richards' is a prison warder and so on − from which we find ourselves plucked and sent into a high-falutin' life in which, for months on end, we see very few people beyond those with whom we work and play. What's

more, the newspapers cover our games. Sometimes we are on
television. We all read about ourselves, see ourselves at play.
It's no wonder we sometimes behave like pop stars.

Today's match was rained off. A large crowd had gathered to
enjoy the sunny weather but the outfield was saturated and at
1.45, without warning, the game was abandoned. Naturally,
Somerset supporters who had driven 170 miles for the game
were furious, and there was a right to-do in the pavilion,
especially when the Surrey officials would not refund entrance
money, Cricket is its own worst enemy at times.

We didn't leave the Oval until 5 pm because we were waiting
to hear news from Slough that tomorrow's game had already
been abandoned.

Supper at the Crown. The local village team trooped in,
telling their stories of the day. It had been wet on the village
green too, and the inevitably hairy and ferocious fast bowler
hadn't been able to stand up. One of his mates said, 'I always
thought bowling was difficult till I saw you bowl, and now I
realise it's impossible.'

Oh yes, one thing more. Viv invited all his West Indian
friends into our dressing room in London and they sat there
chatting noisily with occasional explosions of laughter. It was
apparent that they held Richards in high esteem as a batsman
but that he was among equals in every other respect, and that he
was well aware of it. It was a most joyous conversation.

Monday 23 May

A day off. Training at Taunton: seven laps of the ground and 50
sit-ups. Nearly killed me. Botham, Richards, Popplewell and
the 2nd XI were in, practising. I only trained. I'll have a bat
with the ball machine tomorrow morning.

Joel popped over to borrow my mower and 'Bilko' Waight
called for it later. I interrupted lunch to watch Joel mow his
lawn. He'd said that all the other gardens in this prim road were
short, whereas his stood high with long grass and 'lots of yellow
flowers'. He didn't want a grass collector, just wanted to make
it look respectable. Towering over the machine, he paced up
and down the lawn front and back with serious intent. I
promised to bring some stuff tomorrow to put on the lawn to
stop all those yellow flowers growing.

Botham said he weeded and cut his garden this morning.

He's living with Ollis and Lloyds in Taunton and he added that he expected them to do the shopping and washing up today. I don't think Richards has mowed his grass for a year or two. I think a little man comes round to do it.

Wednesday 25 May

v. Sussex at Taunton (1st day)

I rather think I fell foul of sunstroke this morning! Had a hell of a headache at about 10.30 after spending an hour practising in the sun. Yes, a strange yellow object appeared in our skies and we were even able to field in shirts and trousers. Viv said it was the first day of the season he hadn't felt cold.

Apart from that it was an awful day. Just before we took the field, someone poured orange juice all over Ian Botham. He took an age to change and we went out without him. Inevitably, in the second over an edge went straight to where he would have been.

From this depressing start the day slowly deteriorated. We were in such a poor state that I had to bowl. Yesterday in a benefit game I'd pitched some cunning leg-breaks and this morning Rose examined the pitch with me and observed that there was a dusty patch right on my length. I replied with regret that I had not one length but several. And so it turned out that I bowled two overs of appalling rubbish. My googly bounced a couple of pitches away, to my keen embarrassment and to the delight of businessmen in their bars. It was the sort of mishap at which Botham would have laughed hugely.

Joel says his feet are weary. He's much more himself today, bowling more accurately than previously. Viv fielded marvellously and refused to talk to a South African agent on the phone at lunch ('Tell the man no, no way'). What else? Well, someone on the boundary offered me a sweet at 6.15 pm. She said I looked as if I needed it. It was just a routine day at work and not a particularly successful one.

Sussex 408 for 6

Thursday 26 May

v. Sussex at Taunton (2nd day)

This is our first crisis. It has been a bloody day and we could be here for a while.

I've been out twice today, yes twice in one day. In the first innings I was stumped, swinging wildly at my mate, Barclay. I'd already been dropped twice in the slips (my last three off-drives have all ended up in the slips — why, oh why wasn't the ball machine available?). Also I was caught off a fine edge by 'keeper Gould but the umpire said 'not out' and I stood firm. Gould knew it was out and muttered something about my having wintered in Australia where no-one walks. He's a lovely bloke, though. Then, having survived Le Roux and Pigott, I went down the pitch to hit Barclay, was beaten in the flight, swung like a lunatic and was stumped. A truly awful dismissal.

So there you are — I really had four innings and scored 19 runs this morning. Things get worse, so hang on.

I never used to be out to that sort of shot so my team-mates were surprised. It was foolish, especially as Barclay had just come on and we had all day to bat. I was worried that I wouldn't be able to score any runs off the spinners, especially as I'd already survived that appeal for a catch, so I tried to hit my way out of trouble. I'd have done much better if I'd just kept my head down and fought it out.

Maybe this idea of attacking spinners is too out of character. To be an aggressive player you have to be a man with no regrets.

All the best players seem to develop techniques against spin and they can chip and milk away without taking risks. Old players like Ormrod and Alan Jones and Pilling just tickle on against spinners without you noticing them. I have no such stable approach, no cleverly grown shots upon which I can rely to keep my score moving.

When I was out this morning I sat in the dressing room and said I couldn't play spinners at all except on raging turners when skilful defence rather than domination was required. You'd think after all these years I'd have worked something out. And spinners are only slow medium-pacers really.

When you are out to a terrible shot you feel like apologising to all your colleagues. You end up being grumpy and over-sensitive to insult as your conscience pricks you to imagine, with Macbeth, that the world is full of ghosts revealing the truth about you. As I was taking off my pads I saw a friend glaring in my direction. I turned to him and wanted to know what was on his mind. He was looking at something else entirely.

I spent the afternoon in the sunshine, chatting to Alan Gibson on the far side of the ground and watching our team slowly lose its wickets. Then suddenly we lost our last few men. Trevor Gard was out without facing a ball (as someone observed, 'without taking guard') and Sussex asked us to bat again.

In the second innings I was out for a duck. Last year I failed to score 6 times. I'm very bad on 0. It was a good ball which left me and crept along the ground. Lloyds said it was good and apparently Pigott thought so too, but second slip and the umpire said it came back into me. So, as at Worcester, I was bowled by a ball I thought moved away but which other people thought moved in. Obviously I'm playing inside the line of the ball. Why? I mean, how can I simply be putting my bat in the wrong place?

Yes, it was an appalling day, my worst so far. I suppose it would be dull if one's fortunes in cricket flowed along happily, roses all the way. But it's most discouraging to do badly and, worse, it preys on the mind. Unless runs come soon, it will become an obsession. It's very hard to disassociate one's human worth and one's success with a lump of wood in one's hand.

Sussex 408 for 6, Somerset 223 and 56 for 1

Friday 27 May

v. Sussex at Taunton (3rd day)

Slept in this morning. No point in obeying my usual routine as I couldn't bat today. Stretched with Bilko, then sat sipping tea and reading the papers. *The Times* says I was uncharacteristic in the first innings, the *Guardian* unsympathetically says I failed twice in the day and the *Telegraph* reckons I was out to a cruel shooter in the second innings. Luckily it's the *Telegraph* most cricketers read since it reports on every game and so by studying it, every cricketer can follow the fortunes of every other player in his enclosed world. We play each other so often; we carry in our memory details of each other's strengths and weaknesses. As a batsman I know what opposing bowlers will be trying to do; if they have a particular weapon, I'll remember it from previous encounters. For example, Paddy Clift's stock ball is an away-swinger but he'll bowl the odd, cleverly disguised, slow off-cutter and bung in a surprise bouncer now and again. In this game Pigott will rush in and bowl as fast as he can without any great subtlety and with boundless enthusiasm. Ian Greig will bowl to a full-length, relying upon late movement to beat the bat and slight variations of angle and pace. Le Roux will rush up and bowl full-length away-swingers mixed in liberally with bouncers.

They know me too, of course, having dismissed me several times each and having seen me score a few runs here and there. They will know that I'm vulnerable to slip catches and will strive to keep the ball off my toes. They will probe my off stump until I make a mistake.

Once play began, I nipped home to read a novel in the garden. There wasn't much I could do and it was a relief not to suffer as we collapsed. I returned in time for lunch, when we were 108 for 7, and we lost easily in the end despite Botham's resolute 83. After the game, Rose called for a meeting. About once a season we sit down in a group to work out what is going wrong. Beyond that we rarely have team discussions, only the odd captain's speech before a day's play.

We all had our own theories. It was a mild meeting in which nearly everyone said their piece.

Sussex 408 for 6, Somerset 224 and 190

Saturday 28 May

Long journey up to Bradford. This trip we'll be in a car for nine hours to play four hours' cricket!

Vic drove this time, which is always interesting as he is very mild-natured and tends to drop off into a dream world which doesn't help us get to Bradford. Also he dithers around a good deal and I have to roar 'Attack!' every few minutes. He needs an automatic car, preferably one which knows which roads to take.

We tried to take a slightly cross-country route up through Alfreton, Chesterfield and Sheffield. Naturally, we lost our way. We sent 'Bilko' Waight into a pub to find out the route. He was wearing his usual Australian uniform, T-shirt and shorts, which must have surprised the locals smoking their pipes of a Saturday night in a Yorkshire pub. We had to wait ten minutes for Bilko to return. When he did, it was to explode outraged that 'The ———— billy-goats couldn't understand a ———— word I was saying.'

Sunday 29 May

JPL v. Yorkshire at Bradford
Breakfasted on black pudding, no porridge. Off to a broken down old ground in the suburbs of Bradford on a murky, misty afternoon.

It's a small ground surrounded by bleak, old-fashioned stone stands. I rather like it, ramshackle though it is. It isn't a ground for flowing off-drives; it's a place of grit and earthy wisdom. 'Don't cut before June, lad — smell out the ball' you can hear the stands saying.

Yorkshire crowds are sometimes annoying. Most of them are knowledgeable and humorous (they like to tease Boycott — 'You've got seven, Geoffrey, seven') but today as before, there was an ignorant group that called out rude things such as monkey-noises when Garner was bowling. Garner is a cool customer and he didn't worry about the provocation. Had it been directed at Richards or Botham it might have been another matter. Two years ago, a group at Headingley went on and on about Botham's waist and Richards' colour. I batted with Viv that day and I've never been with a man more angry. He smashed several balls into the crowd with his fury, venting his emotion upon the bowler, his pride surging into explosive activity.

Rose won the toss and Boycott and Sharp opened for Yorkshire. They are such a dramatic contrast. Sharp is a firecracker of a cricketer whose eyes blaze with excitement when he bats. Boycott was as distant as ever, though he joked and shared respectful glances with Richards, Garner and Botham, whom he considers his equals. I happened to see him before the game sitting alone in the dressing room with his cap off, shut off into his own world. He looked very old suddenly and yet on the field he was as sprightly and as fit as ever. It so happened I was off the field when he was out, too, and I watched him sit with his pads on for many minutes, thinking about his dismissal and talking to Illingworth about his intentions. He'd been caught at long-on and he'd meant the ball to go over mid-off. But he's a lovely batsman, so resolutely side-on and so very straight.

He did play a slog today, though. I've never seen him slog before. It was a wild heave at Popplewell and it skidded unwillingly to square leg. It looked wrong. You could see it was a slog of duty rather than of rash pleasure. It was an inhibited slog. His brain said 'Slog' but his body didn't want to. It hadn't been trained for that sort of thing.

I caught a catch today, an easy one at mid-off. My first catch of the season in proper cricket, it takes my average right up to 50%.

They got 164 in their 40 overs. In gloomy conditions, Lloyds and I put on 30 off various parts of our anatomy. I scored 7, not even one run for each hour's travelling, before I straight-drove Stevenson and was outrageously caught and bowled. I hit the shot very, very hard. It was a strange dismissal, an eerie dismissal, because I did not really regard myself as being out. The shot wasn't meant to go in the air and the catch was so outstanding that between delivery and catch it did not occur to me to say 'Oh, drat!' or whatever. It never occurred to me that I'd be out. Even when he held onto the ball, I couldn't altogether accept that this was the end of my innings in Bradford. Still, you can't make a complete berk of yourself, so I walked off feeling rather aggrieved.

After that Botham batted with immense care. He had lost his temper in the field and bowled two bumpers which cost us ten runs, to my expressed annoyance. When he was eventually out, he apologised for losing his rag and said that he hoped his innings made up for it. It did.

Home after a non-stop drive at 10.30, happy and victorious.

Yorkshire 164 for 8 (40 overs), Somerset 147 for 4 (32.1 overs)

Monday 30 May

Benefit game at Ottery St Mary. Plenty of wine about. It's a lovely village down there and a convivial game except that it always seems to rain.

Tuesday 31 May

Game of golf with Viv. He went into the pond in front of the eighteenth green. I went into the same pond off the first tee.

Over to Hallam Moseley's this evening for some West Indian soup (vegetable, chop, sweet potato, dumplings). It was obvious Hallam had been cooking rather than Joel for the dumplings were only as hard as dried mud. When Joel makes dumplings you need a drill to break into them.

Viv joined us for supper from the pot. He was in one of his irrepressible moods and talked about his interest in boxing. He said that the greatest boxers − Ali, Hagler, Hearns, Frazier − were men who had no doubt, men who could stare out an opponent and destroy him even before a fight began. He described Ali's taunting and Hearns' cold stare, adding that these boxers never blinked in the pre-fight confrontations; they never shuffled nor showed any sign whatsoever of vulnerability, fear or respect. They had immense faith in themselves. They could not be broken.

I suspect Viv applies these pugilistic principles to his batting. His whole demeanour from the moment he enters, like Alexander onto a battlefield, is calculated to dominate bowlers. When he cares about the game, Richards' every muscle intimidates his opponents. His face is screwed up with emotion, his body is taut with aggression as Smoking Joe Frazier's was, and his conviction that he will dominate is unshakeable for all to see. His brutal annihilation of Willis which even *Wisden* calls 'a vendetta-like' attack at Old Trafford in 1980 was startlingly reminiscent of Frazier launching at Ali. Richards' face told of absolute commitment to breaking this man once and for all. That is Richards at his best. A competitor to fear, and the bravest of all cricketers.

Botham, by contrast, has no such depth of belief in himself. Cricket is not to him a matter of pride, a test of courage and manliness. He sometimes expresses astonishment that he has taken so many Test wickets and there are times when even he feels it is not much fun to face a barrage of short balls. After his tour to the West Indies he admitted to being shell-shocked, a concession that Richards would never have made.

Friday 3 June

Over to Bath after a two-day rest, for a benefit game. Torrential rain but we played on, oh, we played on. It was very wet so I danced down the pitch and swiped and was stumped second ball. David Allen (ex-England) and Vic Marks bowled them out. It was interesting to compare them. Marks, leaning back as he bowls, luring the batsmen to their doom with his hanging loop, dangling a carrot as wizened old Greek ladies do to their asses heaving under a weight of sticks. Allen, by contrast, with his high arm and pivoting over his front leg, bowled with endless subtle variations of pace and strategy, imparting energy upon the ball so that it jumped off the pitch. Leslie Thomas of *The Virgin Soldiers* was in our team though he did not field, he said he was too ill. And Leslie Crowther turned up to lend moral support (mostly from beneath an umbrella). Bath had several Hoods in their team, rather more, we thought, than the Mafia.

Saturday 4 June

v. Essex at Taunton (1st day)
At 2.15 pm today Denning observed that I could be captain on Wednesday! By then Rose had limped off with a nasty back injury, leaving Botham and Marks in charge. They are off to the World Cup on Tuesday and, as Richards and Garner have already gone to join the West Indies, this could leave me holding the reins. There isn't anyone else.

Last time I captained Somerset was in a 2nd XI game back in 1976. I was stuck in a traffic jam on the way to Devon and I arrived to discover that Bob Clapp had already won the toss on my behalf and had invited Devon to bat on a pitch which rapidly deteriorated. There was only one other able cricketer in the team and he thought he should be in the 1st XI — who, to be fair, had called the groundsman from his roller to make up the numbers that day — and spent the game standing stock-still either at straight hit or at long stop as the case might be. We lost.

Since then I haven't held the reins of power. I think it could be my fate to lead inept teams. A day ago I was seventh in line of succession and about as likely to succeed as Princess Anne's chauffeur. Now I could be in charge on Wednesday at Bristol.

Today, all morning Essex played and missed. At least Fletcher and Gooch played and missed, poor Hardie tickled his first ball and was out. The difference between success and failure can be that small, whether you play and miss or edge.

Fletcher was interesting to watch; he plays the ball very late. He missed the ball a lot but I think that was part of the plan. When the ball is swinging around he plays down the line of the stumps so that if it swings away he misses it by several inches. Presumably he reckons that the dangerous ball is the one that nips back into him, and that is the one he musn't miss.

Essex were 114 for 1 at lunch but it couldn't last. Dredge persevered and received the reward of five wickets as we bowled them out. I caught two slip catches off Dredge, both sharp ones.

We had to bat for an hour. I batted in just a shirt as it was a sunny day. A week ago it appeared as if superstition might be creeping in the back door only half-recognised even by me, for I'd taken to batting in a vest, long-sleeved shirt and sleeveless jumper. Popplewell has been given a clean sweater but refuses to wear it because he feels his old one is lucky. I scorned him, telling him that sweaters couldn't be lucky, all the while realising that I was being every bit as stupid. The pitch was lively and we lost three early wickets to Foster and Phillip, who'd bowled Surrey out for 14 a couple of days before. Foster, tall with a high arm, bumped the ball into the middle of the pitch over and over again. You're only supposed to bowl one bouncer per over, but since the definition of a bouncer is that it must go over the shoulder and I'm a tall bloke, you can bang the ball in time and again to the likes of me on a pitch which doesn't bounce steeply. It's a foolish rule anyway − it should be up to the umpire to prevent intimidation.

Trevor Gard joined me as night-watchman at 6.05, chewing on his gum, and we fended them off. I was dropped once but otherwise played okay. One ball from Pringle jumped off a length and reared over my head. It'll be interesting batting on this pitch on Monday.

Later. A couple more things struck me. Slocombe joined me as Lloyds was out, and at the end of the over he wandered down the pitch and told me he had a feeling of déjâ-vu as he dreamed last night that Lloyds would fail to score. He said he wasn't going to reveal the rest of his dream to me. Can you imagine that? A fellow wanders down the pitch, tells you he dreamed your partner would get 0 and won't say what's going to happen to you. I didn't like the sound of that!

And my batting. I decided to abandon technique altogether. I think all that fancying about with backlift and walloping spinners is a lot of nonsense. I watched Fletcher bat today, and he doesn't bother to look pretty. He just stands with his bat at right angles and glides the ball behind square leg and occasionally past point. He's been doing exactly that for years. It doesn't worry him if it's not classical and that there are a lot of shots he can't play. He just gets on with it.

Essex 262, Somerset 35 for 3

Sunday 5 June

Thunder and lightning all day.

Monday 6 June

v. Essex at Taunton (2nd day)

Wickets are a source of mystery to me. For no apparent reason this 22-yard strip of grass lost its devils over the weekend and rolled out into a slow, reliable pitch. How on earth can it change so much? It makes no sense at all. It sat under covers for 38 hours and emerged entirely different.

Well now, how about this? I'm to be captain at Bristol on Wednesday! This was finally decided when they realised there was no other possibility. Tonight I've been working on my 'fight 'em on the beaches' team-talk by reading Henry V at Agincourt.

This idea of captaincy has provoked a certain restlessness of mind. Whereas I'm usually able to wander in the field, worrying whether I'll have to bat that day and planning how I'd go about surviving, now as captain I'll be studying those around me. I imagine I'll discover a great deal for better or for worse about those with whom I play.

Today's cricket was interesting. The ball plopped off the pitch so that Gard and I renewed our partnership with quiet confidence. We joked on Saturday that they'd have to close the gates on Monday morning when all Taunton realised that Gard and Roebuck were in. We're the two biggest blockers in these parts and, luckily for spectators, rarely find ourselves in together. Both of us are background men, prompting others to deliver their best lines.

I was bowled for 69. Here's how I saw my dismissal. Roebuck advances down the pitch, hoping to drive an off-break; he sees Acfield has bowled a fast yorker, tries to jam down on it, misses and is bowled. Here's how the umpire saw my dismissal. Roebuck charges down the pitch to a full-length ball from Acfield, twists his back trying to steer it to third man, misses and is bowled.

I did hit Ray East, their left-arm spinner, over the top a couple of times but mostly I struggled against him. He's a good bowler who's able to pull down the ball by wrapping his wrist around it, curling it. Like all good spinners, he bowls with a fast arm which means that the ball is bowled with life but not pace. East is a funny man. Every team he plays against recalls some story about him. Our favourite is about the time he played Lancashire on a wet, flying pitch. Realising that it was dangerous to bat, he approached Ken Shuttleworth, Lancashire's fast bowler, and whispered that if Shuttleworth would kindly pitch the first ball up and on the stumps he, Raymond East, would miss it, be bowled and leave the scene in one piece. Up rushed Shuttleworth and delivered his half-volley, which East swung high and mightily over mid-on for four. Shuttleworth glared ferociously and stormed back to his mark. Up he hustled again and, at the moment of delivery, East dived to the ground, flinging his bat away and lying flat as a corpse upon the pitch. From that position he was able to watch the expected bumper fly high and handsome over his stumps!

After I was out, Denning asked if I was ever going to score 100. I haven't scored many. Whenever I approach three figures something ridiculous happens and if it carries on, 100 will become as unapproachable a barrier in my sub-conscious as it is to Geoff Miller.

The pitch will take spin tomorrow and Essex have Acfield and East, two excellent spinners, to take advantage of it. Both men are highly strung, which is perhaps the reason why neither has played for England. I wonder if they regard themselves as failures on that account; does a sadness lurk beneath their sparkling repartee?

This evening Gooch scored 34 lugubrious runs in 33 overs. He must be finding it difficult to excite himself with ordinary county games with no prospect of Test selection. It's no wonder that sometimes these brilliant cricketers find the daily routine of cricket dull and seek their excitement beyond its boundaries. They must sometimes feel like concert pianists only able to play pop tunes in bars, unable to stretch their finest abilities.

A small thing of significance occurred today. We erupted into an appeal for lbw against McEwan, only to stifle it as the umpire raised his finger. We realised he'd hit the ball. The finger was withdrawn. There are still quite a few men in cricket like that, men who simply think it an insult to their professionalism, to the umpires and to their opponents to appeal for anything unless they think it's out. Even I strangled this appeal, perhaps because McEwan is such a fine fellow.

After I was out I went shopping for some rice pudding for supper.

Essex 262 and 112 for 4, Somerset 250 for 7 dec.

Tuesday 7 June

v. Essex at Taunton (3rd day)
First bad decision of the season. It wasn't out, never. Lbw? How can you be lbw to a left-arm spinner on a turning pitch when your foot is down the pitch and probably outside off stump?

It was a moral decision. Umpires sometimes take it upon themselves to impose good batsmanship upon their charges much as moral re-armers hope to impose decency on Society. I took it into my head to sweep across the line and umpires don't like that sort of thing. With some you never sweep because if you miss, you're dead. This fellow wasn't one of those but he raised a finger of condemnation anyway. If I'd been plodding forward in respectful manner I would have been safe, in fact the bowler wouldn't have bothered to appeal. I felt robbed of my wicket but surprisingly maintained a dignified silence even in the dressing room, though I did explain in a bemused voice that it couldn't have been out. Someone should write a book of cricket excuses.

I scored 41. We lost easily, with men throwing their wickets away. Vic Marks was the last one out, caught at long-on! Marks was upset by his brainstorm. He sat glumly in the dressing room, brooding upon his downfall. He's off to the World Cup which means we'll miss him for three weeks. I expect he's worried about being on such a big public stage and that worrying may have persuaded him to go for a swipe when we were rather hoping he'd block.

This evening it emerged that 'Falstaff' McCombe has been asked to be our new scorer. Our current man is leaving, which is a pity since he produced charts of runs scored, balls faced and minutes at the crease which used to get me widely excited because I'd confuse balls faced with runs scored.

Hard to see Falstaff as a successful scorer. No, that's not true. He'd be a most successful scorer but not necessarily a particularly accurate one. He knows little of leg-byes, no-balls or wides, having grown up in the world of lager and kilts.

Here is Falstaff describing his fight to what he imagined to be robbers.

Prince: What, four? thou saidst but two even now.

Falstaff: Four, Hal; I told thee four.

Poins: Ay, ay, he said four.

Falstaff: These four came all a-front, and mainly thrust at me. I made me no more ado but took all their seven points in my target, thus.

Prince: Seven? why, there were but four even now.

Falstaff: In buckram.

Poins: Ay, four, in buckram suits.

Falstaff: Seven, by these hilts, or I am a villain else.

Prince: Prithee, let him alone; we shall have more anon.

Falstaff: Dost thou hear me, Hal?

Prince: Ay, and mark thee too, Jack.

Falstaff: Do so, for it is worth the listening to. These nine in buckram that I told thee of, –

Prince: So, two more already.

Falstaff: Their points being broken, –

Poins: Down fell their hose.

Falstaff: Began to give me ground; but I followed me close, came in foot and hand; and with a thought seven of the eleven I paid.

Prince: O monstrous! eleven buckram men grown out of two!

So far this season I've scored 230 runs in six innings. Nothing to be excited about but not that bad. A sound start to the season for a reasonable English professional batsman. That's what you realise you are in the end, not in a sad way, for it's very difficult to be a good professional batsman. It's just that when you start, your hopes are so high because you were the best in your group and hasty people said you'd be another Colin Cowdrey or some such. Eventually you realise it's not to be, and you have to adjust to the lowering of your sights without being unduly harsh. It must be harder for those who have played for England but without success. Many of them suffer long bouts of failure as they realise that they had a chance and didn't take it. So 230 in six it is. Cricketers always know the statistics, whatever they say.

And I'm to be skipper tomorrow. Somerset phoned through their team to Gloucestershire whose captain, David Graveney, rang back to see if it really could be true. He hadn't recognised some of the names. Oh Lord.

Essex 262 and 242 for 9 dec., Somerset 250 for 7 dec. and 113

4

I Am a Captain

Wednesday 8 June

v. Gloucestershire at Bristol (1st day)
First day as captain.

Upon reflection it was not wise to look forward to today so much. I spent the night tossing and turning, thinking of how I could create a happy atmosphere in which this young team could relax and be successful. I decided to adopt as cheerful and cavalier approach as possible, in stark contrast to my usual demeanour, in an effort to appear confident not only in myself but in those around me. I can remember how much difference it made when I was young to feel that my team-mates and our opponents thought I was good.

And what good did it do? We lost the toss, and after about 40 minutes the heavy realisation came to me that captaincy was not all it was cracked up to be. The large, unsympathetic scoreboard revealed that Gloucestershire were 84 for 0 after 13 overs of Roebuck leadership.

It was the helicopter's fault. 'The helicopter' is the name by which Gloucestershire players refer to Stovold because of the havoc he wreaks to his immediate surroundings. Stovold is either a good player in brilliant form or a brilliant player. His approach to batting is simple this June. If the ball is up to him he whacks it. If the ball is short he whacks it. If the ball is wide he whacks it. If the ball is straight he whacks it. He played a succession of streaming strokes against our fast-medium bowlers and scored 80 in what seemed like 15 minutes but can't have been. In the end he skied Popplewell to be caught by a most reluctant slip who had a long stare around before squeaking 'Mine.'

That set the tone of the day, though we plugged away and slowed them down. I rushed about trying to keep everyone in good spirits and the score within respectable bounds. At least we could feel we were putting our heart and soul into our cricket, and could draw the immense satisfaction this brings.

Eventually they declared at 375 for 8. We'd lost three wickets by the close, including mine to Franklyn Stephenson, a West Indian fast bowler who was playing his first county game of the year. We knew all about Stephenson's outrageous slower ball, how it comes down at about Marks' pace and is almost impossible to detect. A slower ball is truly mastered when the batsman is waiting for it and still can't detect it. This ball looked like a full toss and only as I tried to drive did I realise the ball wasn't there yet. I attempted to strangle my stroke but succeeded only in sending the ball steepling upwards immediately in front of me, much to my horror. Stephenson had time to charge down the pitch and catch it.

There was only one thing to do at the close of play. I announced to the team that this was a three-day game and not a one-day match, and where there was life . . . After that I repaired to the sponsor's tent, hoping that people were enjoying my reign and wondering why everyone was going around with grins on their faces muttering 'fighting 'em on the beaches'. Had I really said that in my team-talk?

Gloucs 375 for 8 dec., Somerset 23 for 3

Thursday 9 June

v. Gloucestershire at Bristol (2nd day)

Second day as leader.

Captaincy seems to include half-hearing conversations which you'd far rather not hear at all. Sitting in the gents this afternoon at a critical stage of our recovery, I thought I heard someone say that a wicket had fallen. I rushed the matters in hand and dashed to the balcony to see if this could be true. I found a peaceful scene, men chatting around in the sun, some reading their papers, others dozing. No sign of desperate activity at all.

The conversation, it emerged, had been between two gentlemen I didn't recognise upon some unknown topic. Captains, I assume, are haunted by the ever-looming prospect of collapse and hear the phrase 'another wicket gone' in every conversation.

We had a much better day today. No longer do I feel like an Indian Chief with plenty of willing Indians but no arrows. We fought back from 74 for 6 to 277 all out. It was 'Dasher' Denning, in his cussed way, and 17-year-old Gary Palmer who sorted things out.

Palmer played some tremendous drives, hitting the spinners over and through mid-off. He is a funny fellow, apparently highly confident and yet not expecting to last. In the final over before lunch, when most of us were rather hoping he'd play a quiet maiden, he lolloped down the pitch and lifted Graveney over his head to the boundary. During the interval, I gently investigated his tactics and discovered that he'd never reached 30 in a first-team game before and wanted to do so before lunch. Denning and I smiled, realising that if we couldn't predict Palmer's tactics, they'd certainly defeat David Graveney.

It was a brave innings by Palmer, guided by the ever-defiant Denning. In a way it's not so surprising that he was anxious to reach 30. In my first game I'd have happily settled for 10, deluded as I was that all first-class bowlers could pitch the ball on a sixpence. Eventually you realise that whoever is bowling stays 22 yards away and it's the ball that must be hit. I learnt that the main jump from 2nd XI to 1st XI is to cope with the faster bowlers and the more deadly spinners.

It is not so difficult to produce a few good performances in

first-class cricket; what is difficult is to be consistently excellent.
It is this need for consistency which sharpens a cricketer's
technique. When I first played I was like Gary Palmer, full of
bright-eyed shots and optimism. I used to hit new-ball bowlers
back over their heads and I used to hook all the fast men.
Since then I've learnt to regard batting not so much as an
exhilarating challenge which is to be met full-bloodedly but as
a hard matter of making runs. The flash and the dash are
abandoned and from hard experience a technique is developed
that is best for securing a few runs.

It was at the end of Denning and Palmer's partnership that
I took refuge in the gents. With our last pair in − Wilson and
Dredge − we still needed 20 runs if we were to avoid the
follow-on. We had to wait for 30 agonising minutes before the
runs were scored, after which Dredge reminded us that he
used to be Frome's opening batsman in his heyday with a
series of hazardous cuts and slapping square drives.

This recovery and the vigorous last-wicket partnership
raised our spirits and we held Gloucestershire at bay in the
final session. 'The helicopter' did not wreak havoc. We
devised some tactics for him: two mid-wickets, a point, an
extra cover and three slips. Also, we put Dredge on to open
the bowling on the assumption that Stovold liked the ball
coming on the bat as fast as possible. Cunning tactics, eh?

Mind you, they didn't work. Not entirely at any rate.
Stovold was slightly more restrained and was out for 34, but it
wasn't our medium-pacers or spinners who dismissed him.

Gloucs 375 for 8 dec. and 115 for 2, Somerset 277

Friday 10 June

v. Gloucestershire at Bristol (3rd day)
Third day as leader.

Evening drive across to Brighton with Colin Dredge to end
a gruelling day. My first game as skipper was drawn. They
batted on too long and set too stiff a target: 330 in 210 minutes
was beyond the scope of a mostly inexperienced team. I tried
to have a go at it but you couldn't expect my opening partner,
Richard Ollis, who is playing for his career in the next couple
of weeks, to try too much, though he opened up as the game
faded to its close.

In fact the game ended on rather a sad note. Ollis and I were playing out time peacefully enough when Graveney introduced Hignell to bowl, as often happens at the end of the game to spare the best bowlers. Ollis lashed out at Hignell, whose leg-spinners are nearly as bad as mine and against whom I was paralysed because I didn't want to get out to him. At 5.30 Ollis was on 99. The Gloucestershire players started to leave the field. As I didn't know the rules, I asked whether we could carry on and Graveney said it was up to me. There were dark mutterings around and Shepherd bowled six bumpers in the extra over before I realised that we should have stopped at 5.30. I hope Ollis will score his first century on a more significant occasion so that it is something he can be proud of.

By the way, Franklyn Stephenson couldn't bowl today, suffering from an injury. It is always encouraging for opening batsmen to see the opposing fast bowler walk on the field wearing gym shoes. We spend quite enough time at the wrong end of a coconut shy as it is. I batted well today, attacking the left-arm spinner, Childs, and cutting him too, but defending stoutly against Graveney, who relies upon line and length rather than flight. It was a relief to score some runs as captain and to prevent anyone saying 'Look how it's affected his game.' In fact I suspect captaincy will help me concentrate my mind.

Rose returns tomorrow. My brief reign is at an end.

Gloucs 375 for 8 dec. and 231 for 5 dec., Somerset 277 and 174 for 0

Saturday 11 June

v. Sussex at Hove (1st day)
Very down, not because of failure with the bat (ball was too good) but because of dropped catch (easy and vital) off Popplewell. It went to my left and was a straightforward chance which ought to have been taken. I don't think I can catch a damned thing to my left. I'm fed up with dropping catches. It's a most disheartening experience.

So I've decided to stay in Brighton for the night rather than travelling with the fellows to Reading for tomorrow's benefit game and tonight's do. I'll drive up in the morning.

This morning it was cold and the sea-front was deserted as I wandered along it for a mile or two to settle my breakfast. It's an open, breezy place, Brighton, with great wide roads and a feeling of health. I like coming here for our games, though the beeches are shingly and the water's too choppy for a surf.

The ground isn't far from the beach and it's a pleasant stroll there in the morning past the Italian restaurant and the bookshop. There's a second-hand bookshop down the road from the ground which I browsed around this morning, after I was out.

It was a dull day's cricket. We lost the toss and batted first, a rarity at Hove. The pitch was dry. We stayed in for 88 overs and scored 181. It was difficult to score runs though I wasn't in long enough to tell. I was out to a good ball from Le Roux, which sneaked back into me. It was a fine ball, especially as the previous three had left me off the pitch. I was happy with the decision ('happy' is the wrong word — let's say I agreed with it). Later, Ollis said that it had nipped back so much it might have gone down the leg-side, which ruined my peace of mind.

Richard Ollis scored 69 today. Ten days ago his career was on a knife-edge. Yesterday he scored 99 not out and, had he failed, he wouldn't have played today. As it is, he was top scorer again and batted extremely well. He's bound to play in the next few games and has a chance of establishing himself in the team. In two days he's changed from a frustrated 2nd XI player to a young man with his name to make and a career in the game. Maybe in two weeks' time he'll be back in the 2nd XI and out of a job next year, or maybe he will go from strength to strength and emerge as a county cricketer. It is all so uncertain.

Apart from my own failures it's been another enjoyable day for the team. We're a young team, not thinking too highly of ourselves and playing together with lots of spirit. We took two wickets for 48 and if I could catch, it would have been three for 48.

Watched TV in the afternoon in the players' balcony overlooking the ground. Backing horses with Breakwell as bookie and losing every time at 10p a go. Time passed well enough.

Somerset 181, Sussex 48 for 2

Sunday 12 June

Morning in Brighton. How foolish to be so upset by a dropped catch. It popped into my hands and popped out again. Immediately, I felt physically ill, sick in the stomach. It doesn't make a bit of sense. Everyone else had forgotten about it in a few minutes and certainly no-one said anything unkind.

Incidentally, a fellow called Dermot Reeve made his debut for Sussex yesterday. He's a youngster I brought to Somerset for a trial two years ago after I'd played against him in Hong Kong. It was a bit galling to see him bowl us out yesterday. *Evening.* Long drive to Reading (awful journey) for a benefit game. Upon arrival went for a stroll in a nearby wood and saw a rabid dog which was charging around frantically. I don't suppose it was rabid really but I headed in the opposite direction with a steady stride in any event. Gary Palmer did a very good impersonation of me batting today. I said I'd copy him if only he'd stay in a bit longer.

Harrowing 2½-hour journey home in the evening, stopping for a pint and a pasty on route. And this is our rest day?

Monday 13 June

v. Sussex at Hove (2nd day)
Either my eyes are going or I was done for a dog's dinner today. My trembling fury has abated but I'm still pretty damned upset by being out to a catch after the ball had bounced.

On my return to the pavilion I clouted an advertising board and roundly cursed a spectator who said I was a bad sportsman. The advertising board had a bad day: it was struck by Barclay, too, after he was out to the first ball of the day. Do you remember my depression after dropping him? How foolish to worry for two days, only for the fellow to be out first ball next morning!

My relationship with the Sussex fieldsmen had been poor all day. Earlier on, I'd plainly edged a ball on to my pads. Nevertheless they burst into an appeal and appeared distraught that it was denied. I went behind my stumps to show them the bat and inform them that you can't be lbw if you hit the ball. As for my dismissal, well the umpire at square leg said I was out and so, after a long glare at the slips, off I stomped. Professional cricketers shouldn't do that sort of thing to each other; it breaks the bonds of trust. Failing to walk is one thing, let the umpire decide that, but saying you caught a catch when you did not . . . But there, perhaps I was wrong. It's not impossible. But it's pretty bloody unlikely if you ask me.

I scored 40 and played some good shots but after I was out we collapsed and they will win easily tomorrow.

Somerset 181 and 112, Sussex 178

Tuesday 14 June

v. Sussex at Hove (3rd day)

In Swansea. Rose was injured again in Brighton and I'm in charge tomorrow. Probably I'll be captain for a week or two now until the World Cup is over. Have to decide who to leave out tomorrow. Must include Breakwell as a second spinner and so must omit Wilson or Palmer or Davis, none of whom deserves to be dropped.

Took some of the troops off to a French restaurant this evening and persuaded one to try escargots. He had no idea what escargots were so I explained that they were a bit like paté. He said he usually had paté so just for a change he'd try the French things. When the plate of snails were put in front of him he looked mournfully at Popplewell and me and announced that he'd 'been done good and proper'. Popplewell and I ate the snails and gave him some oysters. We were in an expansive and expensive mood.

Dredge and I lost our way on the long journey from Brighton to Swansea. We passed the same lorry three times at one stage. And when we arrived in Swansea and booked our rooms and I was about to descend into a bath, reception rang and said we were in the wrong hotel. We packed our bags and wandered up the road to the Dragon or Dolphin or whatever it's called.

One thing about being captain is that you are entitled to a single room. This means that you can return to watch telly or listen to some music or read a book without worrying about anyone else. Usually I share with Marks or Popplewell and this is all very well except that inevitably we wake up at different times — in order, Popplewell, Roebuck and (much later) Marks. It's a relief to get away from the team sometimes. I value their company but not all the time.

Went to bed early, beginning to feel very tired. Long journeys, endless days on the field and general worry about the cricket is taking its toll.

We lost today and I didn't acknowledge the sympathies of the opposing captain.

Somerset 181 and 112, Sussex 178 and 118 for 3

Wednesday 15 June

v. Glamorgan at Swansea (1st day)
4.35 pm. A sunny Wednesday afternoon in Swansea. Pleasant, patient crowd whose only fault is that they walk behind the bowler's arm all the damned time. Some cricketers are more fussy about these things than others (one or two reckon they can't see that far), but it did strike me that with all these men in white coats around, someone should stop the wanderers.

I like playing here with the sea so handy and the wicket so good (not necessarily in that order). There is a poem by John Arlott entitled 'Cricket at Swansea' which begins:

> *From the top of the hill top pavilion,*
> *The sea is a cheat to the eye,*
> *Where it secretly seeps into coastline,*
> *Or fades in the yellow-grey sky;*
> *But the crease marks are sharp on the green,*
> *As the axe's first taste of the tree,*
> *And keen is the Welshman's assault,*
> *As the freshening fret from the sea.*

We are 205 for 5 after 70 overs. Denning was caught behind after the ball bounced. I was with him and I damned well saw it bounce. He did, too, and he isn't a fellow given to deception. Shortly after that I missed a ball from Nash; only the bowler appealed, as is his right. Eventually he received muffled support from the Welsh chorus behind me. On what scant evidence I cannot say, but the umpire said I was out and after a lengthy glare I was on my way. In stark contrast to my fury at Hove, I walked back in a mildly humorous frame of mind and when the crowd asked me how I was out I replied, 'Hard to say. Not caught at any rate.' I was out for 40 in dubious circumstances for the second time in a row.

5.30. Breakwell and Gard are leading an excellent recovery. I've changed back into my whites and am threatening to declare. My team are distinctly disgruntled. Of course I've no intention whatsoever of declaring — let the Welsh fry in the sun — but it's good fun to listen to my team's passionately persuasive arguments as to why tactically we must bat to the close. All of them in the end come back to the fact that my men are enjoying themselves sitting in their shorts and in their deckchairs.

Later. Went to the Mumbles with Popplewell to sit on a rock and watch the waves roll in interminably. In 1975 I came here shattered by my bad form. I scored 148 next day and 158 the day after in the Varsity match. Every time I've come to Swansea since then I've come down to the rocks to seek inspiration. Not that it's done a bit of good since.

Somerset 323 for 9

Thursday 16 June

v. Glamorgan at Swansea (2nd day)
Fifth day as leader.

Broke Brian Close's long-standing record by cursing three people in five seconds. First a fellow didn't stop the ball, then as they ran a single our 'keeper didn't run to the stumps (upon reflection he'd have needed to run 15 yards in one second) and finally our short leg didn't dash in to take the ball. The team laughed, saying they hadn't realised I was harder than Close.

Their last pair were in and proving stubborn. They're still in, and they need 33 more runs to avoid the follow-on. If it's a sunny day tomorrow we won't be able to bowl them out again I don't suppose, unless of course the tide comes in at the right time. When the tide's in, balls make green marks on the pitch. Mind you, cricketers do sometimes attribute abilities to the elements which are rather generous. There was a game in Kent, at Maidstone it was, where a Somerset player seeing the ball suddenly begin to move about said the tide must be in. This caused some surprise: Maidstone is not on the coast.

Colin Dredge and I went out to a restaurant this evening.

On this trip we have 11 players, and a twelfth man who left today to take part in a 2nd XI game. Oh yes, we have a scorer too. That's all, no-one else. And yet is not cricket a game whose perils lie as much in the mind as in the body? We'll have had ten days away from home by the end of this game and in that time young players, and experienced men too, could have suffered crises of confidence. They could be worried about their form, doubting their ability, even affected by some illness at home. And who is here who can help them? It is no wonder that cricketers are sometimes driven to mental self-destruction; when there is no-one around except other players wrapped up in their own affairs, the only thing a fellow can do to attract attention is to be outrageous. I should know.

Somerset 323 for 9 dec., Glamorgan 141 for 9

Friday 17 June

v. Glamorgan at Swansea (3rd day)
Home at last! 13 days' cricket on the trot (it will rise to 21) and 9 nights spent in hotels are at an end.

The men were happy when 5.30 finally came and stumps were drawn. They dashed through showers, jumped into cars and drove off. There had been much teasing all day about the prospects of the evening as wives and girl friends awaited their return. We need not, I think, go into details.

It was a gruelling day on the field. I had enforced the follow-on more in hope than expectation. I didn't really want to bat again anyway, didn't want to risk failure.

We tried hard to bowl them out but it wasn't to be. We dropped a couple of catches (Lloyds and Roebuck) and Alan Lewis Jones, who was out first ball yesterday, stayed in to score 99. I spent the day fielding close to him. It was interesting to watch him change during his four-hour stay. At first he said nothing and batted in an unfussy way, but once he'd settled he smiled at bowlers in recognition of some partial defeat and chatted to fieldsmen. After three hours of propping at short leg, I retreated to block his favourite leg-side shots. Immediately he popped up a catch to short leg. Wearily I trudged up to try again, closing the gate after the bull had escaped.

He said. 'Oh, Lord, you're back.'

'Yes,' I replied.

'It's that sort of day, isn't it?' he said. 'A catch the minute you're gone.'

It was a good-humoured day for the most part (we'll come to the minor part in a minute). Geoff Holmes had to defend his wicket for the last few minutes as the game quietly faded. He got himself into a tangle and started hunting down the pitch, upsetting our benign co-existence. I advised him to stop messing about and to block up. He stoutly defended the next ball and I said, 'Ah, that's the stuff, Geoffrey.' We didn't really want to get him out, didn't want to damage his career at so late a stage.

We took a rather less warm view of one of Jones' colleagues. He was caught off his glove and went to great pains to start rubbing his shoulder. The umpire said 'not out'. I didn't think he should have influenced the decision like that. During lunch, some of the team rubbed a cricket ball on their shoulder to produce a stain which was singularly absent on this batsman's shirt.

And so the game slipped to its ritual close. We spent the last hour rushing about, trying to improve our over-rate. We must bowl 19 overs an hour on average or be fined.

What would the Americans make of cricket? Three days ending in a dull though happy draw. I like these tranquil draws; they're a rare lull between storms of tension that batter at the spirit much of the season. It was a good game, full of tenacious and skilful cricket and with a dash of controversy too. An interesting game in which one fellow was out first ball one day and made his highest score the next.

Somerset 323 for 9 dec., Glamorgan 154 and 193 for 3

Saturday 18 June

v. Derbyshire at Bath (1st day)

Captain again, but my entire day was ruined at 7.15 this evening in the sponsor's tent. Chatting to the Derbyshire players (a bearded, craggy lot) I discovered that the pitches at Derby this year are green and fast; the Derbyshire fellows were saying how enjoyable it would be fielding in the slips once Holding returned from the World Cup and joined their Danish fast bowler, Olé Mortensen. I observed that yes, it would be hair-raising stuff, especially on a green 'un and added that it was a great relief that our game against Derbyshire this year was being played at Bath before Holding's return. It was then that the news broke: Lord's have decreed that Somerset are to play Derbyshire twice this year for the first time in ages. Our second meeting will be at Derby in August. This spoilt any remaining complacency which survived an over bowled to me by Mortensen at 5.45 pm.

Olé is from Denmark, and has a shock of black hair. He says little and his appeal is presumably Danish for 'owzat'. He takes a dim view of fielding and, if he is moved from one spot to another, an even dimmer view of chasing any ball entering his previous domain, reasoning that he could not be expected to re-enter an area so recently vacated. He is, though, a very fast bowler. He hurtles in to the stumps and bowls from wide of the crease, aiming the ball at middle stump and sweeping it across you towards the slips. Steaming in with his flailing black hair, he bowled me just about the best over I've ever received.

The first two balls were of a full length and I played ritually forward and ritually missed as they flashed past my outside edge like Barry Sheene taking a corner. Next ball was short and whistled towards my chest. It flew to the 'keeper and the Derby slips shouted an appeal. I don't think the ball hit the bat on its way. Umpire Alley shared my doubts and said 'not out'. The next ball was another full-length away-swinger which eluded me. Then came a 'harrier', a ball which climbed almost vertically from a length and was taken by Bob Taylor jumping high into the air − a most unsavoury delivery. I survived the over and decided that the best place from which to study Mr Mortensen was the bowler's end. Accordingly, when I faced Tunnicliffe I contrived not to score any singles. You do that by blocking the ball and hitting any aggressive shots very hard. So poor Denning had to cope with Olé (two earlier batsmen had already been swept away by the typhoon). It was only a gale by the time I found myself down his end again, and I survived. Mr Mortensen is a serious man, and we have to face him again.

Oh, one more thing. Geoff Miller played superbly to reach 84 this afternoon. It then occurred to him that here was his chance to score his first first-class century and batting at once became impossible. The same bowling, the same pitch and yet suddenly he could scarcely put bat to ball, so shattered were his nerves. It was an insight into a mental block which plagues a man, an obsession which prevents him scoring a first-class 100. It had all been so simple for so long.

Derbys 289, Somerset 32 for 2

Sunday 19 June

JPL v. Glamorgan at Bath

A memorable, stirring victory today. As we sat in the dressing room after the game, we felt as if we had defeated a superior cause and defied odds our supporters had deemed impossible.

It was a heartening day, the sort which keeps you going for months. We had to score 236 in 40 overs and, urged on by a large crowd, we strode to victory in the thirty-ninth over. Our runs were scored by Denning, Popplewell and Slocombe but the final few were knocked off by Dredge and me. At the end there was much back-slapping and cider-sipping in the dressing room.

It is so much more exciting to win when you aren't expected to. It was the first time we'd taken the field as the outsiders for three years. Only three of us had ever passed 50 in a limited-overs game before. Cricketers don't often get excited by victory — there are so many of them, and so many defeats, too — yet this evening we are full of joy and you can see pleasure bubbling in people's eyes. It was a day when cynicism was swept away.

They won the toss and hit us about, hard though we battled. I slightly messed up the tactics, I think, by bowling Gary Palmer at the end. He was too inexperienced to resist the onslaught; luckily, he isn't a fellow to fall to pieces and he'll bounce back.

No-one thought we could possibly reach 236 and so we scarcely took it seriously at first. I dropped down the order because if Denning and I had opened, our batting would have had all the experience at the top and none down below. As it was, Popplewell and Denning added 80 or 90 in extrovert style. Popplewell was particularly aggressive, whacking the ball over deep mid-wicket and lifting it over cover from time to time. We didn't have any worries because we didn't really think we had a chance.

I sent Slocombe in after Denning was out because of his ability to lift spinners over the top. Barry Lloyd had just come on and he's Glamorgan's most accurate bowler. Slocombe duly hit him twice over his head and, to our delight, Lloyd was withdrawn. In the ground the crowd had been urging us on for hours and even in the pavilion now we began to think we had a chance. Rather than sitting around joking, we began to sit alone and concentrate on the game. Popplewell fell, brilliantly stumped, followed by Slocombe and Breakwell. So it was the gangling figure of Colin Dredge who came out to join me at the crease. We really had no-one else to come, only Trevor Gard and the rabbits.

What a fellow Dredge is! He's only scored a few runs this season, yet twice this month he's saved the follow-on, and today in came the demon of Frome to play an inspiring, wonderfully game innings. His extra-cover drives were scintillating and twice at vital moments he lifted Barry Lloyd over the covers to the boundary. This never-say-die attitude inspired me and I too found some balls to hit to the boundary.

The Welsh bowlers quickly fell apart, bowling full tosses and balls outside the off stump despite their leg-side fields. Eventually we needed 18 in 3 overs. Astoundingly, we had a very good chance. Dredge again cover-drove and then scrambled a few singles. One more cover-drive and we were home, to a huge ovation from the crowd. As Dredge hit the winning runs, I remember yelling, 'Well done, Bertie' and dashing from the field as the kids streamed on.

Our dressing room was a noisy, emotional, colourful place. I don't think any of us had felt such a simple pleasure in victory since 1979. We shared the immense satisfaction of playing in a young team, a vigorous team that had tried as hard as it possibly could and somehow defied the odds to achieve a great victory. Even the oldest and most experienced amongst us found in it something to rejuvenate our spirits.

This evening, an hour after the game, we collected in the sponsor's tent and sat around watching Gordon Prossor sweep away the dust from today's game and peg down covers for tomorrow's pitch. All around us, kids were collecting pieces of paper, empty bottles and old newspapers – the debris of today's match. Our celebrations will be brief. It's back to the grafting tomorrow; Monday morning swiftly follows upon this triumphant Sunday. I have to face the first ball at 11 am.

Glamorgan 235 for 4, Somerset 237 for 5

Monday 20 June

v. Derbyshire at Bath (2nd day)

Back to the harsh realities as yesterday's emotion was cast aside and our ominous position had to be tackled.

There is such an adjustment to be made for each player from batting in a Sunday League game, where the field is spread and each ball is vitally important to the team's hunt for runs, to a quiet Monday morning where you must try to rescue your side with a skilful and tight defensive innings. Your approach has to change so much in twelve hours. One day you pick up your bat more and seek to manoeuvre the ball into gaps, next you go out to bat and try to defend your stumps with every power in your possession. This morning, for example, I angled a ball from Colin Tunnicliffe into the slip area. That's a risky one-day shot, but valuable because there are never any slips. It's a stroke I've developed over the years, and I use it to keep my score ticking over if they are bowling accurately. But today as I glided the ball I looked around and there were four slips and a gully. As it happens, Bob Taylor was standing up and dropped my nick. It was a silly shot, but what is learnt on Sunday is not so easily scrapped by Monday.

That area apart, I batted as well as I could today until a ball from Finney snaked back into me and kept low. It's in my technique to play late, to play the ball off the pitch. Occasionally I'm beaten when a different sort of player will be lunging forward and safe. But you can't have it all ways. I was lbw for 44 and we gradually collapsed. It was Dredge, yesterday's hero, who once again saved the follow-on. After lunch the wicket improved immensely as the sun broke through. When there are clouds at Bath it swings a lot and when they roll away the pitch slows down and the ball moves less.

As I was walking into the dressing room after being out, I saw two or three of the younger players looking surprised and worried. It occurred to me they were surprised I was out and were worried about the team's prospects. I've never felt so flattered in my life! I suppose they regard me as the bastion of the team. Golly, I don't feel like a bastion at all. I feel like a bloke desperately clinging on to his wicket through thick and thin. I must appear to them like an old dependable. They don't realise I'm saying to myself, 'I hope to God I don't get out next ball' every ball.

Dredge injured himself on the field which means that we're now missing eight 1st XI players. Of the regular team only Denning, Popplewell and I survive. As a result Popplewell had to bowl 15 overs unchanged in the evening heat. I never actually informed him of this fact but kept him going by asking for one more over.

Derbys 289 and 165 for 6, Somerset 141

Tuesday 21 June

v. Derbys at Bath (3rd day)
Sitting under an old beech tree in Kingsmead Square, Bath, on this sunny evening, waiting for my favourite basement restaurant to open. Our game finished early (you can guess in whose favour) so I repaired to the simple friendly hotel up the road from the ground where some of us are staying this week. It's too far to travel every day from Taunton to Bath, a hellishly slow journey up hills and down dales and behind lorries. Here I can get a quiet meal somewhere in Bath and wander through the wide streets and amongst the churches and shops and pigeons, remembering all the haunts of my boy-hood here. I saw the Roebucks' old flat in Broad Street. It's been turned into a Probation Centre!

We lost shortly after tea. Our mistake had been to take their last four wickets too quickly, forcing us to bat for two hours under heavy clouds. Their tail consists of a raw-boned Scotsman and a Viking, both of whom regard defending as something cissies do. By lunch Mortensen had swept away our early order, consisting as it does mostly of apprentices. I was out to an away-swinger which was magnificently caught by Bob Taylor in front of second slip. I'd strolled to the ground behind Bob this morning and for some reason watched him carefully on the field. As every wicket fell he jumped into the air with delight, no less enthusiastically than when Botham bowled Alderman to end that extraordinary test at Edgbaston in 1981. Every time we lost a wicket, he jumped to the heavens and dashed to congratulate the bowler.

Denning led a stirring fight-back after lunch in his grittily uncomplicated way ('If it's up there, it has to go, don't it?'), despite which we were 123 runs adrift in the end. Young Gary Palmer failed with bat and Denning said to him, 'It doesn't matter if you make your runs standing on your head as long as you make runs.' You don't have to bat perfectly, you just have to make runs.

Any lingering sadness in our dressing room at the end of the game was routed by 'Falstaff' McCombe bursting in to say, 'Christ, there's a girl outside with the biggest knockers I've ever seen!'

Derbys 289 and 166, Somerset 141 and 191

Wednesday 22 June

v. Gloucestershire at Bath (1st day)

Morning.   Sitting in our dressing room amongst the debris. Piles of cricket cases, boots lying around, pegs covered by wet towels and shirts, helmets and bats in every corner. Not a salubrious surrounding, and yet pleasantly quiet before the herd arrives.

And what will our eighteenth day on the trot bring? Eight first-team players are absent and we're down to the last men on the staff.

As the herd arrives, smoke and hard cursing begin to pollute the air.

Evening.   I won the toss. I used a 2p coin this time. We batted and I changed the order around because of our collapses. This provoked a row with a fellow who argued I was making him bat where he'd fail, which would damage his career. His interests collided with the team's.

Whether it was a reaction to this dust-up I cannot say, but at the crease I went for my shots with unwanted recklessness. I square-cut Lawrence very hard and then drove Shepherd off the back foot to the point boundary. Then I went for a drive outside the off stump and was caught behind for 10. It was a crafty bit of bowling by Shepherd. He could see I was playing too loosely against the new ball and offered me one to drive, swinging away outside the off stump. I fell into the trap.

I spent the morning dozing in the dressing room and the afternoon wandering round the ground with Richard Ollis who'd scored 36 and who should have scored more. I asked him why he'd been out. He said he'd been a bit casual. He said he shouldn't have changed his helmet for a floppy hat. On the way round, I observed Peter Denning chatting to some mates behind a tent. There were indications that he'd been in the tent. He said, 'I'm not here, captain' and I replied, 'Neither am I.' He's had his benefit and intends to enjoy the rest of his career and has developed a habit of disappearing from third man every time a wicket falls to sit in a deck-chair and sip a drink.

We reached 238, a careless effort as this is a much better wicket.

We took three early wickets and would have had more if I could catch. I dropped an easy one, Hignell when he was 30. What on earth I was doing at slip I cannot say, as I am captain. Must be an idiot. Maybe we'll get him first ball tomorrow, too. And maybe we won't.

As a matter of fact I felt very grumpy after I dropped this catch. I was so upset that for the first time as captain I retreated into my shell, said nothing and did nothing. I suppose it was inevitable that this would prove to be a most successful tactic. Not changing the bowlers worked well, because Wilson took two wickets with the last two balls of the day. In the dressing room everyone congratulated me on my shrewd and unbending aggression.

Somerset 238, Gloucs 87 for 5

Thursday 23 June

v. Gloucestershire at Bath (2nd day)

Throughout the morning people bounded in to announce that you wouldn't play for a month in Wells or Weston or wherever they lived. They were stunned that Bath, set deep in its valley, had stayed as dry as a Methodist Chapel in a prohibition. During the day we had a couple of brief showers to disrupt things, in particular to disrupt Gloucestershire's violent innings (Hignell, as round, bearded and tempestuous as Henry VIII, stayed in), but most of the heavy clouds, which were bringing drenching rain to the rest of the West, lumbered over the hills.

And so we passed another day in our boots and whites trying to prise out Gloucestershire batsmen with a dank rugby stand, tents and the Folly castle on the hill gazing emptily upon us. Tomorrow we'll read the stark statistics of the day — Bill, caught Bert, bowled Bob 31, Tony lbw bowled Andy 20, and the rest of it — and forget the wooden atmosphere of this trying Thursday in June.

Thursday night.   Barge trip up the Avon with Somerset and Gloucestershire players plus a journalist or two, organised by Scyld Berry of the *Observer*. Wine and pizza aboard as we chugged a mile or two towards a pub. Had to park (do barges park?) 500 yards from the pub because of the tide. At about this time a torrential storm began and we found ourselves trudging across muddy fields full of cow-pats and crawling under barbed wire fences and through what turned out to be someone's garden. Eventually we arrived, soaked to the skin, at the sanctuary of a pub. Sales of the *Observer* in Bath will, I think, fall after this. Our return journey was completed later in the night and Popplewell, Romaines, Sainsbury and I found ourselves in the same pizza restaurant, filling in the gaps left by our watery but entertaining experience.

Somerset 238, Gloucs 232 for 7

Friday 24 June

v. Gloucestershire at Bath (3rd day)

Home at last! Sleeping in our own beds for only the second time this month. Home after a week in Bath and ten days on the road before that. Tomorrow is a rest day. For the first time in ages, we will not have to stir ourselves to perform with a high level of skill. There are no torrid fast bowlers to be faced, no unreliable pitches, no cunning spinners to be endured.

Our game with Gloucestershire ended in drama. Three-day cricket creates situations in which teams help each other to score runs so that a declaration is possible. For some reason I never quite manage to be batting at these times. I read in the paper that X has been bowling high full tosses or long-hops and the batsmen have helped themselves to lots of runs, and I wonder why I seem to spend my time fending off Marshall, Clarke and Underwood. Well, today I had my chance. They put Dudlestone on to bowl his flighted left-arm spinners. He uprooted my off stump! Whereupon a manically energetic Popplewell strode to the crease and reached 40 before I'd unstrapped my pads. He went on to top 100 in 41 minutes, the fourth-fastest century in first-class cricket history, I'm told.

It was an extraordinary innings. At first Graveney and Dudlestone were generous in flight and field-placing but later, as things slipped, they tried to slow Popplewell down. It was too late – as Ray Stevens sings in 'The Streaker', 'he'd already been interested'. By now anything seemed possible. Graveney fired a ball to the leg-side, Popplewell backed away and fenced it over extra cover's head to the boundary. The next ball pitched in the same place and he swept it to fine leg for four. Then he tugged hugely over the tents at deep mid-wicket. Most of the men were on the boundary by now but Popplewell clouted on, hitting the seamers with short-arm jabs and cracking things past cover. He'd scored 143 by the time he missed one, and we'd scored 230 by lunch, despite taking 40 minutes over the first ten.

It didn't seem quite like that when I was in. This morning John Shepherd bowled seven sweetly conceived overs of swing from which we scored no runs at all. He varied his pace and swing beautifully. One ball left me late and I played and missed it. I said to myself, well it must have been wide, I should have left it alone. His next ball was wider and I held my bat aloft to let it go by, only to see the ball nip back and whistle over the top of off stump, causing considerable gnashing of teeth from bowler and slips. I said to myself, well that was close, I'd better play at the next one. It was just outside the off stump and as I stretched to it, it curled towards the slips. Outwitted three in three.

We set Gloucestershire 305 to win in 195 minutes – not exactly generous, especially as I bowled our quick bowlers a lot. They collapsed after tea and if we'd held a vital slip catch we'd have won. I enjoyable placing the field, with a fellow on straight hit and one at deep point. You don't see men in those positions any more.

On Sunday our stars return from the World Cup and Botham will be captain. It's been a three weeks full of insight.

It's forced me out of my shell and made me more concerned for the welfare of others. I've also learnt that captains must have an incredibly thick skin and not be the sort to worry about their decisions.

Somerset 238 and 299 for 3 dec., Gloucs 232 for 7 dec. and 198 for 7

5

A Hundred at Last – Nearly Two

Sunday 26 June

JPL v. Gloucestershire at Bath
The lovely thing about scoring a century is that it proves
you're the master for the day. Somehow if you're out for 97
rather than 102, people hardly notice and even cricketers will
say, 'He should have scored 100' as if those extra few runs
make much difference. Unless you score 100 you haven't
really asserted your mastery, the innings is not fully matured.
Someone once said (he was an idiot) that batting, like life, consists of three stages: not birth, life and death but in, innings,
out. If you reach 100 years of age, the Queen sends you a
telegram; if you hit 100 runs, opponents congratulate you and
headlines proclaim you.

I was out to the last ball of our innings for 105, caught off a swipe. I haven't scored a century for two years in first-class cricket and have passed 50 thirty times in between, so let me remember all I can about today's cricket.

For a start I batted in a floppy hat as I had last week. I don't think this makes any difference unless it helps relaxation. If you wear a helmet it's likely to put you on your guard as if you are expecting trouble, like wearing a holster in westerns, but then sometimes you are right. Apart from that there was nothing physically unusual in my approach today or in my feeling. I can't remember being unusually fluent or confident before the game. I felt as an actor must feel before every performance. A part of me was saying, 'Oh hell, I must go out there again' and a part of me was trying to create a mood which would reduce my chances of buggering the whole thing up.

Nor did I do anything technically different as far as I can see. At first I picked up my bat only a little as Lawrence was bowling fast and I hoped to guide them to third man. Sainsbury opened the bowling at the other end with his left-arm swingers and he bowled well, so I had to rely upon nicks and tucks to pick up some runs. Denning and Richards came and went. I think it was the dismissal of Richards that gave me my chance to play a long innings. No longer was I batting with a nagging doubt that Richards and Botham were to come, straining at the leash: Botham was already in and Richards out.

I reached 40 and quite frankly I still hadn't played any particularly notable shots. We were 100 for 2 in 22 overs, and by this time Botham had injured his leg and had a runner. Botham lashed out and was eventually caught for 75. I decided it was about time I started to go for my shots and lifted my bat shoulder-high. That was the only change in technique I observed through this innings. In the last ten overs I hit a few powerful straight drives which persuaded Graveney to drop long-on and long-off back. This was an important breakthrough since it meant I could get a single any time I wanted one. I late-cut Shepherd and he said that no-one had done that to him since Frank Worrell. Next ball I squeezed him from off stump to square leg and we laughed as if to say, 'Well, Frank Worrell wouldn't have done that.'

I did hit one good shot to a straight ball from Doughty. It

was on a good length and I waited for it to reach me before dropping my bat and whipping it through mid-wicket to the boundary. 'Big Bird' Garner joined me for the last over and I was on 99. He hit one to gully and said, 'Run'. If Romaines had hit the stumps I'd have been run out. Next ball I guided one for four to reach 100. It was a marvellous feeling and a relief to show people that I could go on with my innings when the time was right.

It's strange that I can't detect any significant difference in today's innings and any of the other 50 or 60 that I play every year. If I could, I might have more chance of repeating it.

Somerset 254 for 6, Gloucs 238 for 6

Wednesday 29 June

Natwest Bank Trophy (1st round) v. Shropshire at Wellington
They've let 13 minor county teams into the Natwest Trophy this year and seeded them so that they play a first-class country in the first round. All 13 lost today, though one or two nearly caused surprises. We were drawn to play Shropshire at Wellington, an awkward game because minor county pitches can be poor and suit diddly-doddly bowlers. We have no diddly-doddly bowlers, only fast, medium and slow bowlers with orthodox actions. Last year we nearly lost at Bedford on a pitch which gave Garner nothing and helped diddly-doddly men considerably.

We have not finished this game yet but our position is secure. Botham and Gard appealed against the light and persuaded the umpire that it was too dark to carry on. From this you might suppose that we were batting at the time. You would be wrong. They were 'keeper and slip. Botham said he couldn't see the ball and that it was dangerous, and he persuaded the batsman to his point of view. All morning he'd been describing his activities as a hang glider, as well as trying to persuade some of us to parachute for him in his benefit year. And here he was, stopping play because it was too dangerous at slip! The irony of this was not lost on his team, many of whom spent the evening walking around as if we were in a blackout, bumping into things with hands outstretched, feeling their way. They had been hoping to get home to their wives tonight.

It's been rather a fraught day. On small grounds like this which are unused to big crowds, players tend to sit huddled in groups watching the game, aware they're being goggled at by hundreds of kids, feeling like exotic fish in a bowl. The pitch was strange, too. Marks and I inspected it before the game and returned to the dressing room to observe that there were a lot of hills and valleys in it and that the ball would bring puffs of dust when it bounced. I added that I'd never scored any runs against Shropshire in my 2nd XI years and so they couldn't expect anything much from me today. Having seen the pitch, the idea of continuing my experiment with floppy hats was scrapped and the helmet polished.

We lost the toss and had to bat first. Denning and I opened, greeted by applause from the crowd and moos from the lowing cattle behind the ground. The first ball lifted and hit Denning's glove. Richards played some majestic strokes and I hung on to score 37 in 35 overs before being bowled by de Silva, a Sri Lankan leg-spinner. I'd had a row with this gentleman a few overs earlier when he'd chucked a ball past me, or as I thought at me, after I'd been given not out caught behind.

Our rain-interrupted day was brightened by the arrival of one of Viv's Antiguan friends, a man called Beckett, a small, silent fellow who was startingly blunt with Richards. It emerged that Beckett is a remarkable man who works with the mentally-disturbed in the Bronx, who can run further than Dennis Waight and do more press-ups than Popplewell.

Somerset 246, Shropshire 125 for 6 (41 overs)

Thursday 30 June

Natwest Bank Trophy (1st round) v. Shropshire at Wellington (2nd day)
Match completed. Popplewell and Marks slept on journey home. Over to Hallam's for two massive helpings of soup and then retired for the day.

I've asked if I can have the tourists' game off to recharge my batteries. I'm very tired, mentally rather than physically.

Somerset 246, Shropshire 159

Saturday 2 July

My request for a rest has been granted. Tourist games are, to be frank, a nuisance. Apart from a University game they are the only non-competitive match we play all season. Tourists use them for practice and counties are hardly likely to waste the energies of their best bowlers.

It is vital to have a break from the strains and stresses of the season. I've been very wound up this month, cursing opponents and spectators and glaring at umpires. Yesterday at a benefit game (on our 'rest days' we seem to be playing in front of thousands of people and surrounded by hundreds of kids) I still felt terribly on edge as if my temper could snap at the slightest provocation.

Brian Rose tried to say I should play against New Zealand because it would give me a chance to do well and enhance my international hopes. I replied I didn't really think I had any international hopes. I could have quoted Eliot:

> '*No! I'm not Prince Hamlet nor was meant to be;*
> *I'm an attendant Lord, one that will do*
> *To swell a progress, start a scene or two.*'

I suspect I could tolerate the pressures of Test cricket, it's the exposure I'm no so sure about. Of course one must want one's character and ability stretched to the utmost, but whether deep down everyone wants to risk Test cricket's harshness I cannot say. Does every MP want to be Prime Minister?

Cricket is full of introverts who find the game itself intensely challenging and utterly frustrating but who feel ill at ease in front of the public. The dressing room, the car and the field are private places. Yes, even the field is a place to relax, it's a place to roam as free as a hippo in mud. It's the bits in between — the autograph hunters or the newspapermen, the cameras and the outsiders — that are difficult to endure. Many of us think like craftsmen and our pride is in our skill, rather as if we were carpenters. For some of us it is a misfortune that our craft is performed on a public stage.

It has been a surprising season for Roebuck. He has scored most of his runs with shots he decided to cut out in April. Wasn't he never going to hit back-foot shots through point again? That's been his best scoring shot. Wasn't he going to pick up his bat high and go for his drives? That didn't last long. Wasn't he going to lift left-arm spinners over the top? Well he's done that a bit, I suppose.

The fact is that this season I've emerged as a back-foot offside player after years as a front-foot leg-side clipper. It's not easy to explain this. Perhaps it's caused by making an initial movement backwards towards my stumps. Over the years I've developed a nervous habit of slipping my front foot forwards as the bowler bowls. It usually heads for mid-off, causing me to lean over to the off-side and preventing straight or off drives since my foot is in the way. Now that I go back more behind the ball, I find I'm in a position to play back drives and cuts without reaching away from my body and, if I do play forward, my foot goes straight down the pitch. Almost by accident my game has improved.

I wonder if any of this has anything to do with changing bats. For nine years I've used a Jumbo until this year, when I've switched to Duncan Fearnley Magnums which are lighter and better balanced. Possibly Jumbos encourage powerful driving but make it more difficult to play touch shots like cuts and sweeps. With the new bat I find myself playing shots I haven't played in years.

I wonder if all these changes are temporary. It is an intriguing game.

Friday 8 July

Oh Lord, Leicester. Brick houses, a bleak and barren ground with stewards who shout at kids as if they were warders in the red brick prison down the road. It has improved a bit this year. The formidable Mr Michael Turner is proud of his success in developing the ground and attracting sponsors, but for all his efforts there is something depressing about Grace Road. It feels downcast, its openness prevents warmth and atmosphere. It is a squat ground, hidden behind council houses and bedevilled by winter winds.

I'm back in business after nine days away from top-class cricket, days spent beneath the hazy sunshine. Most of the time was used cutting down shrubs and trees and grass.

Travelled to Leicester with Denning. We chatted about our

scorers because one of them died recently. He was a large, round man who smoked and drank a lot but whose private life was remarkably colourful. His predecessor, it emerged, was an embalmer in his spare time. Our present fellow drew lots of charts but has decided that work for the Civil Service will be less hazardous. His replacement (not 'Falstaff' McCombe after all) is known only as 'the cardigan' since apparently he used to work in the scoreboard and wore a cardigan as his uniform. He has turned out to be David and a good sort.

I read something interesting in *Echoes From An Old Cricket Field* today: 'Try for once to play a match with one object in view and let that object work incessantly for the interests of your side, and do all you can to promote the happiness of those playing with you.' It is, I suppose, as simple as that.

Saturday 9 July

v. Leicestershire at Leicester (1st day)
Morning. Very nervous, not having played for nine days. I can't altogether remember how it was I scored runs before. How did it happen? How high did I pick up my bat? What was I thinking? What were my feet movements?

Playing every day, I must have developed some sort of formula, but now I can't remember accurately what it was. And even if I could, I suppose I'd be playing from memory rather than coping with each ball with fresh spirit. How shall I play Roberts and Les Taylor? It's a relief Parsons isn't playing. The first two balls he ever bowled to me hit my off stump!

It's as if the season were starting all over again; as if a new mystery tour was beginning.
Saturday night. Off to a favourite Greek restaurant hidden in an alleyway near our hotel to drink some Demestika with Marks. When will I ever learn? Out for 50 once again. It was 6.25 and I was shutting up shop. I'd been on the field all day, fielding for 3½ hours, batting for 2¼ and I was tired. John Steele — 'rustless' to his brother's 'stainless' — bowled an innocuous delivery. I put my bat in the wrong place and was lbw. Had it not been so near to the close of play I'd have attacked Steele. I'd already told Richards of this intention and he had advised

caution − Richards advising Roebuck to be cautious! What a silly dismissal.

It had been a scratchy innings, weak on technique and concentration. Sam Cook was umpiring. He said he'd had a few days off, too, and he was finding it difficult to apply his mind to the game. After an hour or so some rhythm began to return and the bat began to feel as if it belonged to me again. I was lucky to survive that long.

At the end of the day we were in a strong position. We haven't beaten Leicester often over the years so it will be enjoyable if we can win. And yet at lunch we were in total disarray. On a sunny morning we dropped catches and everyone had been swearing at each other and we were disgruntled. During lunch we sat apart or slept or read a paper. Not a word was said. After lunch, for no apparent reason, Botham and Garner bent their backs and took eight wickets for 45 runs. There was no explanation for this turn about, it just happened. I never will understand this game. Now for some moussaka.

Leics 180, Somerset 161 for 2

Sunday 10 July

JPL v. Leicestershire at Leicester

A second unhappy day at Leicester. These fraught days when the team is so ill at ease always seem to occur away from home. In home games the players see each other from nine in the morning until seven at night and then disappear to their families or their pubs. On away trips we hang around together, are happy and pleased and angry with each other, never being able to pull back from team affairs. Inevitably this produces days when it's fun to be part of a team and days when the experience is sour. What on earth is it like in prison, where people are trapped together for years on end?

This evening I went for a stroll around Leicester, losing myself in the back streets before returning to our hotel to listen to some music. I hope that this current low does not cause too much disarray before it passes.

It would have helped to win today. As it was, we lost a vital toss and had to bat on a slightly damp pitch under a cloudy sky. We didn't score enough runs. Rose injured his back again and won't play again this season, so Richards will be our fourth captain in a fortnight on Wednesday, with Botham and Marks being at a Test match.

Somerset 196 for 9, Leics 197 for 2

Monday 11 July

v. Leicestershire at Leicester (2nd day)

Morning. Sitting among the roses, hyacinths and pansies which adorn this ground, among the basking crowd at deep third man, watching the flanelled fools in the far distance. Kids are playing their games all around and yelling 'owzat', running each other out and awarding themselves diabolical lbw decisions. It's a gorgeous sunny day which is brightening up Grace Road and it's a Monday with no particular pressures on the players.

It's much too tranquil a day to waste sitting in the dressing room dozing, doing crosswords or fuelling the jargon of cricket conversation. In the distance Ken Higgs is umpiring because Sam Cook has had to leave to see his wife in hospital. I wonder if any other professional sport tolerates a coach of one team acting as an umpire. Denning has just been bowled. Popplewell is striding to the crease, swinging his arms with lusty intent. I hope we bat all day. It's wonderful here amongst the flowers.

Afternoon. Oh dear, seven men out already and we've only just finished lunch. Our eighth-wicket pairing is interesting, though – Richards and Botham, who has come in late because he was feeling queasy this morning. Richards is batting with a clinical mastery he doesn't often bother with these days. His head is absolutely still, like a Roman statue, and his bat is relentlessly straight. Normally in county games he makes batting more interesting by backing away from the stumps and whacking sixes irrespective of line and length. Today he is demoralising the bowlers by first forcing them onto the defensive and then picking up singles at his leisure. When Richards bothers to take singles, bowlers know they are in for a hard day.

Evening. Much of this afternoon was spent trying to persuade our tail-enders that the longer they stayed in the better. Garner, who slept most of the day, did not oblige but Hugh Wilson defended heroically. Our advice had been founded on the interests not so much of the team as of the team's players who didn't want to fry under the sun for too long.

After Wilson's gallant effort we finished 348 ahead and they'd reached 42 for 1 in 100 minutes by the close. Richards finished with 214 and Botham with 154, both making it all appear as if it were an afternoon tea party. I'm sure they edge the ball as often as I do, it's just that with them the slip-fielder is at deep long-off.

Leics 180 and 42 for 1, Somerset 528

Tuesday 12 July

v. Leicestershire at Leicester (3rd day)
Loud Wurzel music bellowed across Grace Road before, during and after the game. Denning had brought his Adge Cutler and the Wurzels tape, Popplewell had brought his cassette player, and so 'Up the Clump', 'Champion Dung Spreader', and 'Drink Up Ye Cider' and the other anthems of Somersetshire echoed across the land, supported by choruses from the Wurzels amongst us. Our West Indian fraternity, more used to Bob Marley, at first muttered things about there being no beat but in the end they were smiling, won over by the sheet effrontery of it all.

After three painful days, Adge changed the group's mood in moments, and laughter returned. His rude songs and improbable rhymes reminded us of the gentle rolling county we were supposed to be representing. In a few minutes his raucous choruses sent all the secret debates into the back of beyond.

We have a Wurzel group in our team too, men who represent the folk tradition of Somerset. Denning often appears as if, to quote Brearley, he'd recently emerged backwards from the haystack. Gard talks about ferrets and goes hunting, and Popplewell frequents (I cannot say wears) a pair of army dungarees which billow around his legs with a generosity of Victorian furls. These three have taken to being simple, stoical types who are silent, strong and who get on with the job, spurning praise.

Every player in the team adopts some sort of character, a

character which is gradually defined for him by the group. Once that character is settled it is difficult to change — for colleagues suspect there is something wrong with a team-mate who is not fulfilling his role. Spurred on by the Wurzels, we survived our 3½ hours in the furnace outside in high spirits and bowled ourselves to our first Championship victory. It was dementedly hot and for some reason I found myself wandering around the outfield reciting 'We came from dust and we shall return unto dust.'

Eventually off to Maidstone, 3½ hours down the road, driving through London's noise. We found Maidstone but not the hotel, largely because Denning and I couldn't remember its name. Finally we drove out of town in despair, came across a large place by a lake and found ourselves booked in there. This evening, we popped out to a nearby village for a pub meal and a chat.

Leics 180 and 277, Somerset 528

Wednesday 13 July

v. Kent at Maidstone (1st day)
Oh golly, oh golly! Out for 99 to my first rash stroke in six hours (the crowd were patient except for the odd fellow who called out, 'You're worse than Boycott'). I was 25 at lunch, 59 at tea and 99 at 6 o'clock when I fell to a hook, caught at long leg. I should have already reached a rare century but Garner turned down an easy single with me on 99. I could feel a surging despair at that moment, a premonition of failure. Kent's captain Chris Cowdrey woke up, brought in the field and denied me a single which I'd regarded almost as my right after six hours gruelling work under a blistering sun. Suddenly scoring a run became an impossibility. I was panic-stricken as I could see my hopes sliding away. I tried to tell myself to take my time but suddenly my body was ill at ease and my mind jumpy. Somehow it seemed inevitable I'd be out. From the moment Garner refused that single a barrier arose in my mind, a paralysis affected my judgement and my nerve. It was all so absurd. How could it happen?

I wonder what psychological harm this has done. I was more bitterly disappointed than I've been for any previous dismissal in my life. I wasn't angry, I didn't throw my bat or curse, didn't blame anyone or anything. I just sat down in the pavilion and put my head in my hands. It felt as if this was typical of my career, as if I was destined to drain myself of energy, determination and finally of hope. It all seemed to be in vain. Garner was even more upset than me, but it was my fault I lost my wicket, not his.

Viv was very kind afterwards, pointing out that it had been a terrific innings for the team and returning the compliments I'd paid him at Leicester by praising my discipline and effort. But it was such a waste for all that. It was an interesting innings and tonight I realise that it was an innings to be proud of, and it is foolish to despair merely because I'd not made one more run.

My experience at the crease was dominated by another duel with Underwood. He is a pitiless bowler, stamping in ball after ball and rejoicing at every wicket, though he has taken so many – which is probably why he has taken so many. He gives you nothing, nothing at all, simply fires the ball at middle and leg and straightens it up off the pitch, trying to coax an edge to the men crouching around the bat. Occasionally he holds one back and every now and then he bowls down a fast yorker but mostly he nags at the batsmen's defence, hammering away like ancient warriors besieging a castle.

I was dropped by Alan Knott. Dropped by Knott and Taylor in one season! What am I complaining about? He caught me, too, but no-one appealed except square leg, who stifled his shout and muttered, 'Well I'm buggered.'

Went for a swim in the hotel pool this evening to soothe out bruises accumulated during the day, and then out for a meal with Garner and Dredge.

Somerset 256, Kent 7 for 0

Thursday 14 July

v. Kent at Maidstone (2nd day)
Morning.   Went to sleep at 12.30 and woke at 5 am, having slept only lightly. After a long innings the brain is tired but still pumping with thoughts and the body is too weary to relax. Does that sound as if batting for six hours was a regular

business, something done many times, and its lessons are well understood? I've never batted for so long in my life.

It was an interesting experience, mentally and physically. The longer the innings lasted, the easier it became to concentrate. After a few hours I began to feel like an abandoned castle and as if I'd be there for ever. I couldn't see how I was going to be dismissed. From about 3 pm to 6 pm my mind lost its eagerness and its frantic application and simply settled down for a long period of occupation. No longer did I have to resist the more idiotic ideas brought by vigour and imagination. I had no vigour left and imagination had been quashed underneath a heavy pattern of defence. No, it was not difficult to concentrate my mind for six hours, not difficult to get my body to obey its instructions for 320 balls.

Physically it was more of an ordeal. At different times during the day my left arm had cramping pain and my right hand was sore, the first from carrying the bat and the second from hitting the ball time and again. There were a few bumps and bruises too; several bouncers hit me in the ribs, largely because I omitted to sway out of their path. My stamina was not tested; we ran I suppose about 170 singles, which is only about two miles, spread over six hours. It's more tiring simply standing out in 31°C heat from morning till evening without eating. I was too hot to eat at lunch or tea, and merely sipped a cup of tea or two.

At the end of the innings my gloves were saturated, despite taking them off when I was not facing, three shirts were hanging out in the sunshine to dry and the insides of my pads were soaked with sweat. My socks were past their peak, too.

This morning my main problem is lack of sleep. I wonder if I'll recover sufficient strength to play another long innings today or tomorrow. Boycott seems to manage it.

Evening.   Stomach still weak, unwilling to receive food.

A change of fortune today, run out when the bowler deflected the ball onto his stumps from a Richards straight drive. Not much anyone can do about that. Mind you, when Richards ran Close out in similar circumstances, Close berated Richards after the game for hitting too straight!

After I was run out (for 9) I wandered amongst the crowds, passing a rickety old pavilion they call the Tabernacle, and sat on the boundary listening to conversations. We've been in the field most of this burning day and at 6.15 we had to go into field again. Our batsmen were not sufficiently skilled, Richards apart, to cope with Underwood's relentless accuracy on this pitch, though most of them lost their wickets to desperate attacking strokes against Johnson's off-spin. We had time in the field to drop three catches, two of them sitters; and time for someone to straight-drive onto the opposite stumps, time for Garner to grab the ball, grab a stump and appeal for a run out, only to realise that he'd held a stump and ball in different hands! A bellow of 'Bird, you are a ———— !' erupted around Maidstone.

Off to a pub this evening; I've had my bats for this match so I might as well have as hearty a night as health permits.

By the way, Garner is hitting outrageous sixes in this match, several of them clearing the poplar trees on a hill far beyond the boundary. I thought he said he was 'done swipin' '.

Somerset 256 and 173, Kent 150 and 27 for 1

Friday 15 July

v. Kent at Maidstone (3rd day)
4½-hour drive home from Maidstone, arriving in Somerset tired out at 8.30. Off to the Crown with some Australian friends for a steak.

Lost today, due to poor bowling and dropped catches. Exhausted all day. Suspect Wednesday is still taking its toll. Hands sore and stomach weak, possibly suffering from heat exhaustion. On the field almost the entire game. I'm withdrawn from the benefit game on Sunday to rest in the shade.

I've been eating badly: no breakfast, no lunch because of heat, only a cup of tea at four o'clock and in the evening nothing more than a salad. It isn't enough to play cricket on. Joel had four helpings of sausages and mashed potato and baked beans for lunch today. He said this was what they used to give him in New Zealand and he couldn't bowl fast on it.

And so ends another eight days away from home. At least we were in better spirits by the end, sung back to life by Mr Cutler and his Wurzels. We haven't seen a cloud in eight days, which is terrific except that if it carries on much longer we'll be sloping around in the field like French Legionnaires with blisters.

Somerset 256 and 173, Kent 150 and 280 for 7

Saturday 16 July

v. Surrey at Taunton (1st day)

Arrived in the dressing room after I was out to observe Trevor Gard asleep under a billiard table, a position he'd apparently occupied since 11 o'clock, and Joel Garner prostrate in his corner, snoozing. The rest of the team were watching the Open golf on TV. Just another day at work with each man concentrating on his job where necessary and slumbering the rest of the time.

As soon as I was out I went into a back room to read the paper and sip some more tea as Richards imposed his mastery upon the bowlers. Yes, as the greatest batsman of our era went out to bat, I preferred to sit in the back room sipping tea.

I did return later to watch him building another of the majestic innings we take for granted. His defence was secure, almost teasing. His forward defence reminds you of Nelson Piquet driving a Ford Popular. He played two strokes today off Clarke which I will not easily forget. He whipped fast rising balls off his hip with a straight bat through square leg to the boundary. There was almost no movement. He hooked Clarke, too, even though there was a deep mid-wicket. Have you seen Clarke bowl? You can't hook him to deep mid-wicket. It's not possible. Moreover, if you do, he's likely to respond with a ball that rises and whistles past your jaw. With his freakish action (apparently his shoulders are double-jointed) he can suddenly bowl a ball which rears up to you where his previous balls had only threatened your stomach. He bowled several to me and I was lucky to fend them off without being caught at short leg or silly point. And yet Richards risked hooking without a helmet. It was an example of boundless courage, of an absolute conviction of mastery.

I hit, if hit is the right word, 58 in 58 overs today. It was a good innings, played with a straight bat. Again I scored most of my runs on the off-side through cuts and drives. I was out to the first ball I'd missed for two hours, which was a bit much.

It was a friendly day's cricket. Most county cricketers still play in good spirit. I've only been roundly cursed by two men in ten years (though my batting has provoked many comments directed at the stars above us). I've never seen anyone run out because he was gardening or heard anyone appeal because he was picking up the ball to return it to the bowler.

Somerset 342 for 6

Monday 18 July
v. Surrey at Taunton (2nd day)

Off to the Crown for a meal. Joel had said he'd be cooking this evening, but when I popped in he had four big black fast bowlers lying on his floor (Clarke, Armstrong, Ezra Moseley, Joel Garner). There is a plague of fast bowlers in English cricket all of whom 'love de bumper'. Of the counties only Lancashire, Nottinghamshire, Northamptonshire, Sussex, Warwickshire and Yorkshire do not have a very fast, coal-black man to strike terror into batsmen. And most of them have a South African, or Pakistani. Add that lot to the English fast bowlers and you'll see that this game is becoming increasingly physical. Unless you can cope with fast bowlers, you won't survive in first-class cricket. If word gets around that 'X is shell-shocked' or 'Y doesn't fancy it', as soon as they come in the fast bowler will be summoned. The bush telegraph is very effective in cricket.

I've heard old players say that they only used to face a dozen or so bumpers a year. I had that many in the last half-hour this evening. I wear a box (did I tell you I forgot to put on my box after lunch at Maidstone?), a thigh-pad, a helmet without visor, pads and a chest-pad to protect sore ribs. The game has changed; it has hardened. The time is coming when batsmen will feel naked if they enter the fray without these contraptions.

Clarke was lethal this evening. He put in a silly point, a short leg, a very close backward short leg and a close gully and made the ball rear up into my gloves over after over. These were not bumpers within the one-bumper-an-over rule laid down by Lord's. They weren't above shoulder-height but they were all rising and all nasty. Lloyds and I managed to survive, feeling that courage was at least as important as skill in batting these days. I suppose I was, if not frightened, at least shaken. I certainly wanted to be at the bowler's end. It does not pay to have too much imagination when facing bowlers like Clarke — you tend to think of the mass of teeth and blood if a ball hits you in the mouth. It is an intimidating experience, playing fast bowling, it's dangerous and thrilling. If your courage stands up you feel proud, more of a man. I could see in the dressing room that everyone thought Lloyds and I were very brave. But they didn't know what fear was hidden in the mind, denied expression more by pride than courage.

Trevor MacDonald turned up to watch the game. He is writing a book about the social influences on cricket and talked to Richards for a long time. West Indians are the most substantial of today's cricketers; fellows like Richards, Lloyd, Holding and Roberts are aware of their standing as representatives of their nation and race. One of the main influences driving the West Indies on has been the belief that they must give their supporters something of which to be proud, so that those in St Paul's and Brixton can hold their heads high amidst racial intolerance. I don't think any other cricketers feel such affinity with their followers, I don't think other cricketers feel such responsibilities. It is significant that the tough core of Lloyd's team have strongly rejected the bribes of 'blood money' to go to South Africa. That's what Gregory Armstrong is doing here; he is manager of the West Indies rebels in South Africa and hopes to sign Richards and Garner. He won't have any luck.

I'm 41 not out this evening and we'll have to hit out tomorrow which is a nuisance.

Somerset 342 for 6 dec. and 79 for 0, Surrey 253

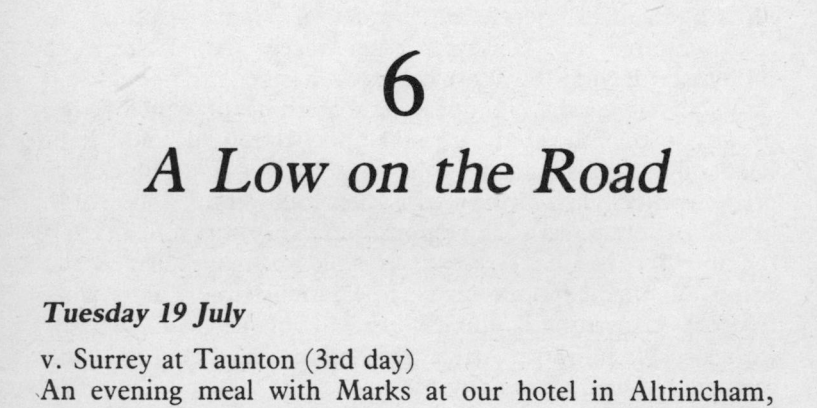

6

A Low on the Road

v. Surrey at Taunton (3rd day)
An evening meal with Marks at our hotel in Altrincham,
preparing for tomorrow's second-round Natwest Trophy
game at Old Trafford, and chatting about the strange mixture
of tragedy and absurdity which surrounds this game and its
lifestyle.

There are cricketers who wander around saying, 'I've lost
it', there are others who wake up one morning unable to face
the ordeal of bowling, unable to pitch a ball on a wicket. There
are cricketers who feel a joyous emotional release when they
reach home and the pressures of another day are over.
Cricketing has more than its fair share of nervous and manic
depressives. Insecurity lies close to the heart of the game, and
it's not everyone who is sufficiently phlegmatic to say that
'Fortune knows We scorn her most when most she offers
blows.'

And yet it is so absurd. Every ball we wander in with the bowler then stalk back to our mark, in and out, in and out like the seas. Off you go to a game after a big breakfast; you stretch, you have a knock-up, you sit and read the papers, you have a cup of tea, you half listen to a team-talk and then you wander out to the field, wondering what's for lunch. What is it that causes us such frustration? Nothing, I suppose, except that we take it too seriously and our failures too much to heart.

We drew today's game. I was out for 48. It was a good game in so far as declaration games can be good. Their last pair hung on.

Somerset 342 for 6 dec. and 223 for 7 dec., Surrey 253 and 252 for 9

Wednesday 20 July

Natwest Bank Trophy (2nd round) v. Lancashire at Old Trafford

> *'Where care lodges, sleep will never,*
> *But where unbruis'd youth with unstuff'd brain*
> *Doth couch his limbs, there gentle sleep doth reign.'*

I'm not entirely unbruised and I deny that my head is un-stuffed, but I did sleep the sleep of the just on the journey home from Manchester.

It was brave of me. Vic was driving. On the way to Old Trafford he'd stopped behind what appeared to be a line of traffic but turned out to be a succession of parked cars. On leaving the ground he didn't notice a white fence in front of us and drove straight through it.

It was a strained but victorious day and we are through to the quarter-final. I batted for 53 overs until the winning hit had been made and scored 43 not out.

Do you realise I haven't caught up with the overs for three weeks?! At least this is a terrible pitch. Its appearance recalled a series of saucers sitting next to each other with cracks in between them, like a jigsaw puzzle. Every ball blew up puffs of dust. It's terribly frustrating for batsmen to have the ball dying forever on the bottom of the bat rather than hitting the meaty middle. On a pitch like this we should have chalked the bottom of our bats like billiards players do.

The pity of it was that there was a large crowd willing their team to do well, hoping for an exciting game. What's more we were on television. I hope they had something funny on the other channel.

Mine was a poor innings. Peter Lever had been recalled because Lancashire have suffered so many injuries and he pitched the ball up. Since I've spent the last few days fending off Thomas and Clarke, I went back to most balls and wasn't at all ready for swinging half-volleys. Still, we won.

About the only entertaining moments today came in a conversation with Marks early on our journey home. He talked about David Lloyd, a bright, shrewd man who has survived the years of upheaval at Lancashire but who says he's had enough and intends to retire at the end of the season. Apparently he holds the theory that opening batsmen must not score too quickly off change-bowlers. They must keep thumping the ball to fieldsmen to soften it up, but not score too many lest the opening bowlers come back. He asserts with particular fervour the notion that an opener's duty is to study the ground and to see where the nearest piece of concrete is, because 'nothing buggers up t'ball like concrete'. Apparently he has a list of grounds where concrete is readily available. Once, when Clive Lloyds struck a massive blow over the sight-screens into the flats behind Hove, Lancashire team-mates roared their approval, only to hear David Lloyd say, 'That's the best concrete shot I've seen for years.'

And so our season is still alive. We will draw Sussex in the quarter-finals. We always do.

Lancs 163 for 7, Somerset 164 for 2

Thursday 21 July

We did draw Sussex at Hove.

The papers are calling me the tortoise. Well, who won the race, the tortoise or the hare?

Went to 'Falstaff' McCombe's to watch the replay of yesterday's game. Horrified to see this anxious, fretting, stooped figure that they kept calling Roebuck. It's appalling how many of your most private mannerisms are caught, exaggerated even, by television. I see now why Peter Tinniswood describes me as Mrs Roebuck of the biscuit shop.

It was appalling. My batting was okay in a poky sort of way but my mannerisms have damaged my ego considerably. I remember being with Vic the first time he saw himself on television. He'd always imagined his off-drive flowed and supposed that he ran purposefully since that was what it felt like. He was stunned to see his crouching drive and his crab-like running style.

The commentators noticed that I talked to myself as the bowler was running in to bowl and, since the game was so dull, speculated on what I might be saying. This morning, everyone in Taunton was asking me what I said as the bowler was running in to bowl. As far as I can recall, I was muttering nothing more romantic than 'Wait for the ball. Wait for the ball.' I wish I'd been reciting 'Tomorrow, and tomorrow, and tomorrow'.

Sunday 24 July

JPL v. Hampshire at Taunton
With thunderclouds mounting behind the Tone, our cricket today had an unusual atmosphere as if we were compelled like some Hitchcock victim to act in a deranged way by forces beyond our control. Demented things heaped upon each other in quick succession: run-outs, bumpers, sixes, rain, applause and so on.

Marshall bowled very fast, with three slips and a gully in a 20-over game. I was out for 0 but Viv hit some staggering strokes, repeating that whip off his hip he'd played against Clarke. It was worth the entrance money alone. We won easily with eight overs to spare. If I'd stayed in we'd have slipped in with five balls left and everyone would have said well done!

I did make one technical change today. As the pitch was hard and fast and bouncy, I stood more upright than usual to cope with a steeper bounce. It didn't bloody well work though.

Garner has had his hair cut and resembles a prisoner from *Gulag Archipelago*, a book he reads during his more gloomy moments.

Hants 93 for 7, Somerset 97 for 3

Tuesday 26 July

Benefit game at Knebworth House. Drove there via Frome to pick up Dredge, a fellow of many qualities, not including navigation.

Played with a bloke from the Lord's ground staff who had only one arm. He opened the bowling with inswingers, caught a good catch in the outfield and, although he didn't bat, I gather he scores plenty of runs with wiry cuts. He isn't the only astonishingly brave fellow I've seen. In the Somerset under-15 team I played with a fellow with no legs at all, he had tin attachments below the knee. And there are men like Milburn and Pataudi, who defied terrible injuries, and Chandrasekhar, who not only refused to be beaten by his withered arm but actually came to regard it as an advantage. Sometimes as a professional you forget how many thousands of kids there are who would dearly love to have your place.

This is our last trip away from home. We're off for nine days, so I cancelled the papers and milk, turned off the hot water and emptied out my fridge.

Wednesday 27 July

v. Northamptonshire at Northampton (1st day)
The facts.   It's 6.15 pm and we're hanging on for dear life. Well, I am at any rate. Jerry Lloyds is smashing the ball over the place. Mallender comes in to bowl. The ball is short of a length and outside the off stump. Roebuck plays back. The ball keeps low and nips into his pads and onto the middle stump.
The case for the prosecution.   Why the hell did he play back? Didn't he see all day that the ball was keeping low? It's a typical Northampton pitch and however hard Mallender hammers them into it, they'll always keep low. So why did he play back? He was asking for trouble.
The case for the defence.   I've scored 1150 runs batting like that this season. Am I to abandon that technique merely because the pitch is particularly slow?
Verdict.   Yes, of course you are, you clot. There's a thousand runs in this pitch for any batsman who plays forward every

ball. And you, a reasonably experienced, intelligent human being, played back in the first over.

I didn't score many today.

Northants 336 for 9 dec., Somerset 39 for 1

Thursday 28 July

v. Northamptonshire at Northampton (2nd day)

Wandered around the back alleys of Northampton this evening, stopping for a hamburger in some basement café, and then sat on a wall outside the hotel watching the cars go by. Most of the fellows were in a pub — 'Bilko' Waight had announced that he intended to do something different this evening, and we'd supposed he'd bought tickets for the opera or something, but it turned out that rather than sitting in the hotel bar he was going to a pub up the road — but I wanted to collect my thoughts in solitude.

Almost every season I sink into a trough of despondency which lasts sometimes a week, sometimes a day. For some reason I seem unable to last from April to September without a bout of morose self-examination. I can sense a growing upheaval within and I'm afraid it will not easily be stilled.

It is inevitable, I suppose, that the trough usually occurs when my form is bad. It is strange that I am doing rather well at the moment and nevertheless feel disturbed. I batted with fortitude at Maidstone and scored 100 runs in the last match against Surrey. There's hardly been time to worry, and from a cricket point of view there is no sense at all in this turmoil.

And yet it is building. Worse, we have eight more days away from home, living on top of each other, sleeping in the same hotel rooms, travelling, playing, training, fielding and eating all together with scarcely any outside influence, as if we were a group of monks who eschewed the world and its people. There is going to be no escape from the rigours of our life on the road for one week. Most bad things that happen to a cricket team happen on away trips, when our lives are dominated by our ephemeral gifts. I can return home after a game at Taunton and put on a record, pick up a novel and not care a jot about events down the road. Away, it is on top of you all the time.

Well, tomorrow I must arise and go to Northampton's

cricket ground, surrounded as it is by red-bricked terraced houses, dominated as it is by bleak, empty football stands.

Stephen Booth makes his county debut in this match. I call him Heathcliff, since we rescued him from the bowels of Yorkshire.

Northants 336 for 9 dec. and 50 for 1, Somerset 337 for 7 dec.

Friday 29 July

v. Northamptonshire at Northampton (3rd day)

They should dig up these pitches. They're killing fast bowlers.

Well, it's been another wretched day. They set us 273 in 160 minutes and we declined to go for them. I wanted to, since I've adopted a couldn't-give-a-damn attitude, a mood which disguises a growing vulnerability. It's an affected attitude, hiding the fact that I care too much. I went for my shots and dashed up to 40 before Richards ordered us to defend.

This evening we dragged ourselves up to Manchester, a 2½-hour journey, including an interminable traffic jam on the motorway.

I scored 55 not out and this ought to have revived my spirit. It hasn't. I booked a single room and had dinner with Marks. I was hoping to talk to him but a couple of the other fellows joined us and so we chatted about nothing in particular.

I feel as if I am motoring from depressing place to depressing place with no sense of purpose except to bang my head against the same old stone wall. I've dedicated myself to being good at cricket and simply cannot do it, which is immensely frustrating. What's more, in my efforts to succeed I become irritable and tense, characteristics I rarely show in my winter's teaching in Australia. If that is what playing cricket does to me, why the hell do I continue with it? What's more, why do I allow myself to get into this state? I suppose it's because it's the only damned thing which means enough to me to cause frustration, irritation and gloom. It's the only thing which stretches, tantalises and tests my personality. That is why it's so bloody disappointing that I cannot crack it. I feel like admitting defeat.

Northants 336 for 9 dec. and 273 for 5 dec., Somerset 337 for 7 dec. and 110 for 0

Saturday 30 July

v. Lancashire at Old Trafford (1st day)
Off alone into Manchester to see a play at the Royal Exchange
(an intimate, extraordinary, theatre-in-the-round). It must be
heartbreaking for actors steeped in experience to play to half-
empty houses. Not that there were many at Old Trafford this
afternoon for Richards and Clive Lloyd.

I told Vic this morning that the world was still rather bleak
but he didn't really hear me and tonight everyone is rushing
off in their different directions. This season started like the
other nine but it's fading in a clatter of disappointments. I
can't believe it is good for my character to be subjected to so
many baffling failures of fulfilment. And yet it is surely worse
to run away from it by seeking some more serene lifestyle. It's
Catch-22: cricket alone drives me to distraction, and when it
drives me to distraction I wonder why on earth I play it. I'm
stuck in a swamp, being sucked down and waving my arms
around in desperation, hoping that someone will notice.

Before the match I sat by the nets and a colleague lashed a
drive straight at me. I don't suppose it was intentional but I
think he could have apologised and asked if I was okay.

I scored 2 and was lbw (plumb). After I was out, I went for
a stroll around the back of Manchester United's football
ground and then wandered to the far side of the ground to
watch the game. We had to field this evening but we bowled
poorly, especially Richards, who couldn't pitch his off-breaks.

We are losing.

Somerset 185, Lancs 104 for 1

Sunday 31 July

JPL v. Lancashire at Old Trafford
Read in the *Observer* this morning what Richards said to
Baptiste a few years ago. Baptiste was despairing of ever
succeeding at Kent and recalled that 'Richards called me to his
room one evening and told me what he felt like when he was a
failure. He kept telling me that my name was Eldine Baptiste
and that I had to fight for it and by the time he'd finished two
hours later the tears were running out of my eyes. I can cope
with failure now.'

Plunged into depression. After the game and amidst torrential rain, I wanted to drive home to break out of this rut. I intended to return on Monday morning to continue the three-day match. It just seemed necessary to do something. In the end I splashed only a little way down the M6 before realising the senselessness of it all. I stopped in a service station and rang up Falstaff, who was in Taunton. We were cut off and later I rang again to discover that he'd set off for Manchester.

Back at the hotel I went for a stroll round Hale and Altrincham; I sat on benches mulling things over. Mostly I was churning over in my mind the reasons for playing cricket. It's not for love or for enjoyment but out of habit and because it pays well. And to prove my superiority over rivals. None of them particularly honourable reasons. I started this business full of noble ideals and now I plod along, fretting and strutting my hour as a poor player upon this stage. And yet to pack it in would be to admit defeat, as if I'd only scaled halfway up my Everest.

Falstaff arrived and appeared in my room with Marks at 11.30 or so. In the corridor I heard him enter a wrong room and heard his loud Scottish accent say, 'Oh, I'm sorry, dear.' We chatted far into the night, trying to work out what had slipped.

Lancs 132, Somerset 7 for 0

Monday 1 August

No entry.

Tuesday 2 August

I must reconstruct these last few days.
Monday.   It is, I suppose, ironic that on my lowest day I did not write anything at all. The very point of this diary is that it should fully reflect my experiences as a cricketer and yet I ignored it when I should most have used it.

Monday was a poor day. Charging about the country with ten cricketers and a scorer, trying to live up to a high level of expectation and performance, had been a burden. I wanted to disappear for a week, or for a month, and yet was expected to 'keep buggering on'.

In the dressing room I gave no obvious sign of despondency. I still teased Heathcliff about black puddings and the others about the usual things. I didn't field, though, just lay down and dozed, complaining of a sickness in the stomach which I could nearly feel. In the evening I wandered around the hills, still juggling things in my mind, wondering whether there was any sense at all in any of it. I decided to abandon my cricket career and start afresh with something less tormenting. I wanted to be able to relax, to be sociable, to be more human — it's in there somewhere but one has to suppress so much of it to win the battle. Then suddenly you realise the battle is not worth winning.

I wanted to be as I am in the winter, and as I cannot be during the season. There's no threat in the winter, I cannot be undermined. Nothing can go terribly wrong and there's no need to tense myself to avoid cruel failure.

The strange thing is that, striding through the hills and villages on Monday night, all this seemed absolutely obvious. I did not doubt that this analysis was sound. I could see no sense whatever in hammering away at this game, nor did I want to play it in any other way. People say, 'Why don't you relax and just enjoy it?' Relax? Enjoy it? What on earth would be the point in doing it in that spirit? It's the battle and the struggle which makes it worthwhile. Good God, relaxation and enjoyment are so irrelevent when you are committed to something. Anyhow, I can't see any value at all in playing cricket — it is an indulgent life — unless you are committed to doing it properly.

I realised all this as I walked and concluded that the commitment was correct, that it was not worth doing otherwise; but I also decided that it was time to admit defeat and to give myself something else to have a go at.

I don't know if deep down I believed I could throw in my hand, though. For one thing it would have been bloody inconvenient. For another, what else would I do? I suspect I wanted someone to talk me out of this Reggie Perrin-like break. But I wasn't play-acting.

Tuesday. This morning I had a chat with Viv. In his different way he has been in an emotional cauldron these last few days, too. He was impressive, finding words and ideas to match his passion. He said sometimes people can be like a house with a fierce dog outside. Do you go into a house with a fierce dog outside? No, so how can these people expect anyone to help them? He said it wasn't a matter of cricket, there is no sense in blaming cricket, it is what people do to themselves that causes their turmoil.

We talked for an hour and a half. I've never known Richards more convincing and yet even at the end of the conversation, I still could see no sense in persevering. It still seemed ridiculous to carry on banging one's head. It still seemed a worthless existence, an empty experiment with a character which did nothing for team-mates and ignored the acres of ability which could contribute something more constructive.

It occurred to me that if Viv could not talk me around, no-one could, myself apart. And so before lunch I went for a stroll around the ground with Vic Marks. Upon reflection, this is when a light began to appear. We sat on a bench on the far side of the ground and laughed about things. Vic was supposed to be convincing me that one must persevere. As it was, my competitive instincts were aroused and I won the debate. We concluded that it would be a jolly good idea to pack in cricket. We laughed at this discovery; we'd rather hoped to reach the opposite view. We agreed that not only should I retire but he should, too!

Humour returned after this. It wasn't so much strength and self-respect that fortified me but rather a realisation that what I had lacked had been that sardonic sense of humour which offers a shield against the severest blows.

It had rained all morning. After lunch the weather began to brighten up. Sadly, this meant we might have to play cricket, a pity since it was a terrible pitch and we were losing. No good at all for the average (I could tell I was returning to my normal self − I was beginning to worry about my batting average) so Vic and I decided that the only thing to do was to get changed and try some slip catches and run around the ground. If this didn't bring rain, nothing would.

It didn't. I went to the bat low down because I was still weak and Vic and I survived for two hours. Vic said it was interesting to see at close range how skilful I was defending against spin. I was out in the end to an unplayable ball and we lost with half an hour to spare. Tonight we dashed down the motorway to Brighton for the Natwest quarter-final with Sussex. This season's darkest moment has been survived — with a little help from my friends.

Somerset 185 and 155, Lancs 355

7
Towards a Semi-Final

Wednesday 3 August

Natwest Bank Trophy (quarter-final) v. Sussex at Hove
Almost involved in a terrible accident on the journey home.
After nine days away, Dredge and I were hurrying home,
adding to the 7000 miles we've already driven this summer.
We were caught behind a lorry with seven cars following in its
slipstream. I decided to go. Off I went, encouraged by Colin's
'Take em all'. Suddenly a car careered round a corner ahead. I
had nowhere to go. The road was narrow and the other
vehicles were huddled up against each other. There was no
point in braking, so I thrust the car into third and roared on,
diving in front of the lorry with inches to spare and amidst
flying pebbles, dust and a screeching of brakes. It was a
harrowing few seconds. More cricketers will be involved in
road accidents unless something is done about all these long
journeys.

We won our game easily today. Sussex were obviously suffering a collective collapse of confidence. Suddenly people who are held in high esteem were scoring no runs. You can see that they have no faith in each other or in themselves. They were 26 for 6 and all out for 65 for no very good reason. It was a day when they'd have got out to their grannies bowling underarm.

I scored 8 and was given lbw. I don't think it was quite out. If the ball hits the pad and bounces back up the pitch it means it was travelling straight when it hit the pad. If, on the other hand, it scarcely touches the pad and skids off to fine leg, I don't see how it could have been going onto the stumps. Mine went fine of long leg. It didn't matter much, luckily.

After the game Botham drove to a waiting aeroplane to fly to see his wife, who is ill. The rest of us climbed into our cars for an eagerly anticipated couple of days away from cricket.

Sussex 65, Somerset 69 for 3

Friday 5 August

Spent last night at Popplewell's country retreat, chatting to Popplewell, Jill and Nigel Felton. Felton was at Millfield after me and we shared some R. J. O. Meyer stories. Felton mentioned one about the time Meyer had opened the bowling at Lord's for the Gentlemen against Australia. When Bradman came in, Meyer called out to Freddie Brown that he wanted an eight-one field on the leg-side, a request which Brown, who was aware of Meyer's eccentric, not to say scurrilous reputation, granted. First ball, Meyer ran up and delivered a very fast beamer straight at Bradman's head. Bradman swivelled and hooked it through all the fieldsmen on the leg boundary, whereupon Meyer walked back to his mark and called to Brown, 'Orthodox field, please.'

At Millfield, Meyer once asked his groundsman to erect a large board with a hole the size of a golf ball in it on the roof of his house. For many mornings thereafter the groundsman arrived at dawn to see Meyer hitting golf balls at the board. Suddenly one morning, Meyer announced that the board could be removed and that he'd granted the school a full day off. He had hit a golf ball through the hole.

This morning I went into the ground with Felton, Denning

and Davis to have a go on the ball machine. My form was poor and we stayed working away for 2½ hours, at the end of which I was happier with my game.

I had lunch at the ground with Falstaff and Dennis Breakwell, who had gone fishing yesterday. Falstaff said the fish were only in danger from him if he hit one of them on the head when he was casting. He added that he had caught a duck which had taken a fancy to the bread on the end of his line. He tried to release it and it was shrieking in terror when two old ladies walked round the corner and assaulted him for cruelty to animals. He found himself wrestling with a shrieking duck and being peppered by two appalled old ladies. He didn't catch any trout after that.

Saturday 6 August

v. Northampton at Weston-super-Mare (1st day)

Oh, golly, the Weston-super-Mare Festival has started. They've erected some tents, cut the grass, mowed a strip and we are under way. Things have improved. The dressing room used to give you splinters and the towels were flimsy, the food was for rabbits and the outfield was as bumpy as Jack Nicholson's face. They've obviously worked hard to improve facilities and the wickets are much better. But we still send Falstaff off for fish and chips at lunch, and today Heathcliff ordered 20p's worth of chips, good Yorkshireman that he is.

As the season begins to draw to its close, our team is taking on a certain manic air. It started before the game. It emerged that Botham had lost the toss and we had to field. As 11 o'clock approached, our room became increasingly noisy with lumps of sugar and bread rolls flying around and all sorts of laughter and manhandling going on. Suddenly a voice full of dismay announced, 'They're out there', whereupon the fun stopped and out we trudged.

I asked Heathcliff if this is what he thought first-class cricket would be like. He said no, he'd imagined that men sit around and talk at least some of the time about cricket.

I spent my day in the field, occasionally roaring 'They're out there!' Also, Popplewell and I took it into our heads to impersonate each other's batting and bowling at mid-on and mid-off.

Off we went for lunch at 1.15 and again for tea at 4.10 (Mrs Webb has taken to providing banana sandwiches for me — wonderful lady!) and finally at 5.40 they declared, leaving Ollis and me to survive the awkward last 40 minutes.

Northants 405 for 5 dec., Somerset 21 for 0

Sunday 7 August

JPL v. Northamptonshire at Weston-super-Mare
Rose early to drive to County Ground to practise on the bowling machine. Our coach, Peter Robinson, gave me 150 balls and I left for Weston-super-Mare feeling much more confident.

In a way our whole club is geared towards success in the Sunday League. Many of our cricketers rely upon instinctive flair rather than carefully developed technique and have the good eye and powerful forearms required by 40-over games rather than the disciplined technique of the longer game. It's these games that fill the coffers and the time is coming when clubs will prefer to employ an effective hitter than a dedicated craftsman.

Arrived at Weston at 12.15 to find our small ground brim-full of chatting people, most of whom had paid their entrance money for a change. The club has erected a wooden fence to supplement the tiny Hadrian's wall which surrounds the ground and over which the young and the miserly have hopped for decades. It was a surprisingly subdued crowd, partly because they closed the cider tents for a while and partly because we won so easily.

Northants only scored 123, with Richards in particular bowling very well. He sends down these slow-medium things with subtle variations so that the batsmen don't quite know if he's going to bowl a fast one or a slow one, and can't set themselves accordingly.

Denning and I hit off the runs, which silenced the crowd even more, especially those holidaymakers and the grandads who'd brought the kids hoping to see Richards and Botham. I didn't play too badly although the pitch was helping the seamers. I played too much across my front pad and was squirting the ball through square leg. But I scored 50-odd not out and felt more in control than I have of late.

Northants 123, Somerset 125 for 0

Monday 8 August

v. Northamptonshire at Weston-super-Mare (2nd day)
Dressing rooms are amazing places. After I was out I peered around our room to see what everyone was up to. A couple were sat on seats, half watching the cricket, half browsing through papers. Someone had nipped off to buy an ice cream. Richards, Garner and 'Bilko' Waight were asleep on benches, using pads as pillows. Lloyds was lost beneath some headphones, miles away. Popplewell was reading a novel with fierce determination. Trevor Gard was sitting with his pads on and smoking a cigar. Dredge was darning his trousers. Life only returned when the tea arrived and half of it was devoured before the unlucky batsmen were allowed to leave the field.

This afternoon I went for a stroll around the stands, where I bumped into R. J. O. Meyer. He hadn't been to Weston-super-Mare since 1948 but said that nothing much had changed. He recalled a game here on a turning pitch in which he'd gone into join his captain at 8 for 5. They decided (as they would) that the only thing to do was to hit out. Mitchell-Innes was brilliantly caught first ball and Meyer hit the next three for six.

I once worked for Meyer in his new school in Athens, a place full of organised chaos. Lessons were given on staircases and even in cupboards, or so it seemed. At lunchtime, as we munched our tiropeta, 17-year-old girls would play five-a-side house soccer and boys would have volleyball and basketball matches in the school's small back yard. I found myself teaching English to Greeks who couldn't speak English; I could not speak Greek. For respite we took a staff cricket team to Corfu, a trip which ended in a riot (see *Slices of Cricket*). Sometimes of a Greek night, Meyer would talk about the great cricketers of his era, telling of Sydney Barnes ('The greatest of all bowlers — every ball looked like a beamer, then the full toss, then a half-volley until as you lurched forward it dipped wickedly and jumped past your gloves'). Also he'd advise me on the techniques of underarm bowling. He demanded that I bowl underarm in a Varsity match, but I didn't dare to because I didn't think that D. B. Carr would be too pleased. Cricket in 1983 would, I suspect, be too unimaginative for RJO.

I was caught out off my glove down the leg-side today, a tame dismissal and rather an unlucky one. I scored about 23.

Northants 405 for 5 dec. and 69 for 1, Somerset 267 for 7 dec.

Tuesday 9 August

v. Northamptonshire at Weston-super-Mare (3rd day)
Weston seems to be a place where old friends turn up to brighten our day, which is just as well as the slightly vacant atmosphere of this ground, full of holidaymakers, is drowning our enthusiasm.

Anyhow, Bob Clapp rolled up. Bob is a tall, angular fellow who played for Somerset for a couple of years and still holds the club record for taking most wickets in a Sunday League season. We used to play together years ago in the 2nd XI. In fact it was Bob who was supposed to pick me up for my first 2nd XI away trip in 1970. I was told to meet him at 8 pm outside a pub called the Something and Something, or was it the Something Something? I couldn't remember. My parents roamed around Taunton, anxiously searching for Mr Clapp. It was by the merest chance that I bumped into him emerging from the Crown and Sceptre at 10.30 pm. He had not, he said, planned to leave before then at any rate.

Today Bob recalled the time we played in Poole when people kept wandering across the pitch looking for the zoo; and where a certain Richard Dinwiddy bowled the first ball of the match straight over the wicket-keeper's head. I was an impressionable youngster in those days and a little surprised at what I found in 2nd XI cricket.

A year later Bob and I, together with an inaccurate fast bowler called Michael Hare, took a boat out along the Thames before a morning's play in Henley. There was a bank in the middle of the river with a small gap in it. I rather fancied we could slip our boat through the gap. Bob said we couldn't. We tried. We failed. We were marooned on that bank until ten to eleven, when finally we wrenched ourselves clear with some sticks. And the time, playing on a bad pitch, when we'd seen Commander Moylan Ash-Jones, RN, push forward. The ball rose over his head from a length, bringing the observation from his partner of 'Up periscope'.

We drew our match today with Richards, batting lower down because of his wife's illness, saving the game. I was out to David Steele, who had been hit into the chestnut trees time and again in the previous game by Graham Gooch. Apparently he called down the pitch to Gooch that you weren't supposed to knock down the conkers until September.

I scored 31 today then watched the World athletic finals in our damp dressing room.

Northants 405 for 5 dec. and 182 for 4 dec., Somerset 267 for 7 dec. and 278 for 8

Wednesday 10 August

v. Yorkshire at Weston-super-Mare (1st day)
Yorkshire arrived changed. They've played here before.

There is something different about Yorkshire cricket. It's as if their structure was more formal than anyone else's, as if the youngsters must obey a hierarchy without which it is presumed they would fail. They're not trusted to survive without constant supervision by their elders and betters. Perhaps this is why some of them have not developed as much as expected. Other counties no longer tolerate, let alone require, apprenticeships from their players. These days, if you don't succeed immediately you don't survive. And yet at Yorkshire it appears that youngsters who immediately do well are watched warily as if they had committed some unnatural act. Moxon scored 100 on his debut last year and then disappeared from sight as if he were a Russian novelist whose memoirs had just come out.

Boycott treated us to his usual routine this morning. He's developed a systematic way of preparing himself for a day's cricket, a shrewd idea since these habits help discipline the mind. He came out, dressed as always in his immaculate whites, at 10 o'clock to do his stretches in front of the pavilion, swinging his arms and testing his legs. Then he wandered to inspect the pitch; after all he might have to face the first ball of the match. Back he strode to the pavilion, greeting Richards with his angled grin and his comments upon his season. At 10.15 he re-emerged with his pads and marched towards his team-mates for some practice. He wanted to find his rhythm.

Boycott scored 83, an untypical number if not an untypical innings. If he gets past 50 he usually scores 100 without necessarily dominating the bowling. What's more he was out stumped. Boycott stumped! Pounding the field but not penetrating it and unwilling to go over the top, he advanced down the pitch, was beaten in the air and surprised as the ball turned sharply down the leg-side. It is one of the crosses that Boycott has to bear that his is the wicket that everyone most wants to take in cricket. The reason, I suppose, is that he's the fellow who most unfailingly values his innings and loses it with the most sorrow.

Yorkshire 286

Thursday 11 August

v. Yorkshire at Weston-super-Mare (2nd day)
Interrupted drive home this evening to pop into a pub with David Foot and Bilko. We talked about Botham's determination to become England's next captain. It'll take a mountain to stop him, especially if he can start taking wickets again. I wonder if he will ever be like Macbeth, a brave warrior bedevilled by burning ambition?

Today I was out for an edged four. I was lbw playing all around a straight half-volley. I had clipped the ball before off my toes and it had struck short leg on the head; he was carried off after a long delay. Next ball I tried the same shot and missed. It was a bloody awful piece of batting. I can't understand why my front foot won't go straight down the pitch but angles towards extra-cover, cramping a free flow of the bat. If you play across straight balls you can't expect to score runs.

This disappointment was slightly assuaged by Boycott falling for a duck this evening. Yes, Boycott out for 0! He was caught at short leg off Mark Davis, our left-arm seamer. He didn't really want to go, but off he went with a shake of the head. I don't think I've ever seen Boycott out for 0 before. It doesn't happen often, and it was so unexpected. His shots are so grooved, his game so chiselled that it never occurs to you he's going to get out. When he hits the ball it doesn't bumble along the ground, it rolls along it. It is as if all his movements were sculptured.

After I was out I sat in the dressing room, watching my team-mates react to their dismissals. Whether he scores 100 or 0, Denning sits down, unstraps his pads and lights a cigar. Popplewell is usually furious, especially if he's been out to a defensive shot which frustrates his battling personality. Richards can be stormy, causing a hasty abandonment of the room, or he can be silent with a hint of dozing annoyance. Botham usually laughs as if it matters not. He never regrets anything he's done. Today Marks and Dredge were both in high dudgeon that they'd lost their wickets to tame catches at short leg. Both would rather have been out in some more valiant way. Our second innings should be interesting.

Yorks 286 and 91 for 6, Somerset 164

Friday 12 August

v. Yorkshire at Weston-super-Mare (3rd day)
Out for a duck to a good ball.

My last few scores have been 1, 12, 23, 31, 4, 0 — not a distinguished series. I must score some runs soon or else I'll be in a bad patch. You know when you're in a bad patch. There seem to be 17 fielders. You expect to be out every ball. The pitch has demons, fieldsmen creep in ever closer and your body simply won't do what it's told. It's not quite that bad yet but it's heading that way.

There is no respite when you are out of sorts, no break in which you can either go fishing or work hard on your weaknesses. Every day you must come out to face the music.

This season I'll bat 60 times in rigorous, competitive cricket and each one must be a fresh challenge or I will fail. It is not easy to be full of vim every day. I can feel fatigue creeping into body and mind. A decent meal and a good night's sleep will recover the body but it is not so easy to replace lost nervous energy, especially when you're spending your time on the road and each day brings you another innings.

Yorks 286 and 177 for 8 dec., Somerset 164 and 153 for 6

Saturday 13 August

v. Derbyshire at Derby (1st day)

Afternoon. Two of our team are batting. Garner and I are off to the nets as he wants to practise his drives. Heathcliff is off somewhere with his girl friend. Slocombe is next man in and he's sat in a chair vaguely watching the cricket. The other seven of our party are lying around sound asleep, heads on pads or towels. I've never seen a team so white and drawn. These fellows will do their professional duty but the barrage of travelling and concentration has taken its toll. Tiredness is a predictable reaction to mounting daily pressures. Men in the trenches feel weary after a shelling, having lived on the edges of their nerves for hours. County cricket is rather like trench warfare at times; the qualities you most need to survive are graft and endurance.

Night. Luckily we were able to bat nearly all day. I forgot to say I was out for 13, carelessly fiddling outside the off stump. This evening I stayed at the ground for a few drinks with our fellows and the Derbyshire lot. For some reason Colin Tunnicliffe, a humble man, is a folk-hero up here to the singing hordes in the popular stands. Perhaps he represents everything that is honoured in this county much as Denning does at Somerset. Marks, my room-mate, went to bed at 8.15 tonight.

Somerset 273, Derbys 5 for 0

Sunday 14 August

JPL v. Derbyshire at Heanor

In stark contrast to yesterday's doziness, this afternoon we strained and scraped as we tried to rescue our lost position on this tiny, absurd ground. Whereas at Derby it was an effort to summon sufficient energy to watch the game, here we were cursing and battling throughout.

And the setting was so different today, too. Yesterday there were a few dozen people dotted about, lending an almost country-house atmosphere to the game. This afternoon the ground was heaving with noise and people; players were hemmed in even after the match by hundreds of kids hoping for autographs.

Tomorrow we resume our game in Derby, no doubt before a sparse Monday morning crowd. After today's defeat we must recover our enthusiasm and after the sapping of emotion we must somehow find fresh spirit. In two days' time we play Middlesex at Lord's in a cup semi-final. From an empty Derby racecourse to a packed Lord's. I hope the next two days don't damage our hopes too much.

We lost today because we didn't score enough runs on a ground with a 40-yard boundary. Even Trevor Gard hit a six. I didn't, of course, but then I had to face Mortensen and Holding on a pitch which was a bit damp at first, but which flattened for their innings. I'm afraid I believe that every pitch improves immediately on my being out.

Holding is known to professionals as 'whispering death'. His run-up is so fluent as to be nearly hypnotic and his feet scarcely make a sound on the turf as he runs. You can hear most fast bowlers stamping as they run in but you can barely hear Holding at all. He's a beautiful bowler, you don't mind getting out to him. And he rarely hurts anyone as his classical action allows the batsman full sight of the ball.

Our dressing room was quiet after the game and I slipped away as quickly as possible. About the only thing to brighten up the day was an old codger in the crowd behind us who kept calling out, 'Thir you are, thir's a fieldsman thir. They can place a field, can Somerset. They know their cricket. Thir's allus a fieldsman in the way.' This fellow never lost faith, despite all the evidence to the contrary.

Somerset 219 for 8, Derbys 220 for 2

Monday 15 August

v. Derbyshire at Derby (2nd day)

We did surprisingly well today. Only Alan Hill scored many runs for them. He's an extraordinary player. He waves his bat around and appears to have no hope of scoring runs. In fact he's like many cricketers who don't have many shots and aren't pretty to watch but have immense determination. He has the guts to battle it out and is a damned difficult bugger to shift.

He lifted Derbyshire to 160 for 4, when Garner suddenly changed the game with an extremely fast spell. An umpire turned down an lbw appeal that Garner considered plumb. The next ball flashed past the batsman's nose, whereupon Garner announced that all his deep fieldsmen could come in 'up on the bat'. For five overs thereafter he bombarded the batsmen as destroyers bombard an enemy coast. This spell was not rewarded by wickets, but it transformed the game and we dismissed Derbyshire for 199. We were 112 for 2 at the close with Roebuck 46 not out and hugely relieved to have scored some runs at last. My confidence was helped by reaching 40 yesterday and batting is not such a treacherous business any more.

Somerset 273 and 112 for 2, Derbys 199

Tuesday 16 August

v. Derbyshire at Derby (3rd day)
We're totally unprepared for tomorrow's semi-final. Tonight we dashed down the motorway, trying to forget the reluctant ritual of the last two days. The team is depressed from its damp days, tired from its treadmill of cricket and entirely out of sorts as it approaches tomorrow's match. I've never felt more exhausted nor less keyed up before a big match. It cannot be sensible to play so much cricket, it reduces the amount of life we can give to each game.

I expect Middlesex are in much the same boat. They've had a hard slog all season in the Championship, though I suspect it is easier to survive a long run of three-day games if you are on top of the table. We have been exhausted by the sheer mundaneness of this match.

Tomorrow, somehow, we'll have to inspire ourselves to concentrate every ball, walking in and being on our toes.

I scored 94 before playing on to Tunnicliffe. There was a hundred there for the taking but something went wrong once again.

Somerset 273 and 233 for 5 dec., Derbys 199 and 186 for 4

Wednesday 17 August

Natwest Bank Trophy (semi-final) v. Middlesex at Lord's
We won a thrilling game in the final over which Botham blocked. The scores were level and we'd lost less wickets.

Botham had led a courageous recovery from 52 for 5 to 222 for 8. It was the best innings I've seen him play and included only one wild stroke; a true captain's knock. At the end he stormed from the field, waving his arms, and in the dressing room exploded with the emotion he'd so uncharacteristically controlled through 48 overs at the crease. Even during tea he sat silently, ignoring the usual mayhem around him. It was an extraordinary effort.

Popplewell was almost hysterically joyful, too, immediately after the game and indeed throughout the journey home. He had restrained his aggressive instincts to play a gutsy and match-winning innings.

Our last close semi-final was in 1978, a traumatic game against Essex. That day I left the field white as a sheet from the intensity of emotional effort and, to avoid the delirium of the dressing room, escaped into a backroom where I sat quietly hidden in an armchair. Today I did not feel all that jubilant, possibly because my role in the game had finished hours before. I was more relieved than anything that we were through.

I didn't watch much of the game after I was out. Since I curse all the time when I'm watching a tense game, I thought it advisable to wander around behind the stands of Lord's. I bumped into Hallam Moseley, who has moved back to his London home. After that I went to buy some Weetabix and nuts at a shop in Edgware Road. I didn't need any Weetabix, let alone any nuts, but it took me away from the intense struggle about which I could do absolutely nothing. Upon returning to the dressing room I found Rev. A. R. Wingfield-Digby (at Oxford when I was at Cambridge) ensconced in an armchair. We had a hiccoughing conversation, interrupted as it was by frequent curses or claps. Wingfield-Digby denied that he had changed religion three times to extend his years at Oxford; he sat with me watching Marks and Botham hit out, suffered as Garner was adjudged run out and celebrated as Botham blocked that final ball.

We'd had to score 222. I was fifth out at 52, trying to cut a wide one which lifted a bit. It had been a hard, noisy period at the crease. Middlesex's players stirred each other up, calling down the pitch to Wayne Daniel and Cowans. These fast bowlers tore in, hurling themselves at the batsmen. Daniel bowled very, very fast. It was a most pulsating hour at the crease, a rousing confrontation between bat and ball. Richards' response to this was typically forthright. He simply set about smashing the bowlers to smithereens. He hooked Daniel — how could he do that? — slashed Cowans and drove both. He hit 23 in a few overs, all the while shouting down the pitch, 'Hang on in there, professor, hang on in there.' He was steaming, meeting the most fierce ball with a harder hit.

And yet while I was batting I found it hard to concentrate. Despite all the emotion I still didn't feel able to devote to my batting my full powers of care and attention. Possibly I was upset that we'd lost so many wickets so easily. I felt we were letting each other down, which was foolish, and a certain fatalism crept into my game. Hard as I tried, I could not quite capture the mood I'd had, for example, during the Bath Festival when it all seemed so important that we won. It was in these moments of disillusion that I lost my wicket, though I don't suppose I'd have played the ball any differently.

As I unstrapped my pads I muttered darkly to myself. It was evident that a deep disappointment clung to the room, as if people felt ashamed that they hadn't matched the challenge of the day. But Botham lifted this sombre mood with his massive innings.

And so we reached Lord's for the fifth time in six years. We are supposed to be involved in first-class cricket for 31 out of the next 33 days. Does that make any sense? Do Liverpool play soccer games day after day before an FA Cup Final? There is talk of organising a rota system so that everyone can have a rest, hopefully helping us all to recover sufficient wit to respond to the challenges ahead.

Middlesex 222 for 9, Somerset 222 for 8

8

Trench Warfare

Friday 19 August

My couple of days' break was rudely ended by an unwanted appointment as Minister of Transport. Lloyds usually organises our travelling details but he was in London. Popped into the ground early to arrange a list of who travelled with who. One or two surprises emerged:

(1) Gard couldn't take his car.
(2) Richards and Garner were playing in Bath and wanted to take their cars on from there.
(3) Lloyds and Botham were already in London.

Despite these handicaps a list was made. I went home satisfied that my job was done. An hour later a phone call interrupted my efforts to drop off to sleep; within another hour, 15 more phone calls disturbed me. From these it emerged that:

(4) Slocombe wanted to take his wife and so had no room for Davis.

(5) Davis had forgotten to pack his kit into the van.

(6) Bilko wanted to take his girlfriend, Graciella.

(7) Bilko had crashed his car.

(8) Popplewell wanted to take his wife and couldn't travel with 'Falstaff' McCombe in the van as a result.

(9) Falstaff had gone on strike as he was now expected to travel with Gard who hadn't seen his wife for a month and wanted to leave at 7.30 pm which was too late for Falstaff who rather hoped to arrive at the hotel in time for a pint of lager.

(10) Marks and Roebuck were being rested for Wednesday and so must travel together in the same car.

(11) Marks and Roebuck both had to take their cars because there were no other vehicles available.

Eventually up to London and off to a favourite ramshackle Italian restaurant for some peace.

Saturday 20 August

v. Middlesex at Lord's (1st day)

Out? Out? Caught behind? Missed it by a yard. Middlesex only appealed half-heartedly – they're top of the table. I was cutting and the ball from Cowans rose and left me. There was no noise, no reason to appeal, let alone to give it out. Caught behind for 33, having played really well.

Popped back behind the pavilion to watch a game of real tennis when I was out and generally wandered amongst the sizeable but quiet crowd. What a different atmosphere from a cup game. People sitting restfully watching the events of the day unfold without feeling any particular partisanship. Much less hustle, bustle with stewards and announcements and oohs and aahs. In the dressing room people were mostly watching cartoons on television or dozing around.

You would have thought Middlesex v. Somerset at Lord's would be a sharp, keenly contested fight, especially as Middlesex are top. But it was not a tight day's cricket, nor a satisfactory battle between two determined, vigorous teams. It was a weary endurance test between two groups of men who have had enough of it all.

This evening I travelled on the Underground to see *Noises Off* at the Savoy. It was hilarious.

I passed 1000 runs for the season in Championship cricket today.

Somerset 249, Middlesex 106 for 4

Sunday 21 August

JPL v. Middlesex at Lord's
Another slightly demented Sunday League game. I don't know if it's the effect Lord's has on us (Denning, refused a drink in the members' bar because he wasn't wearing a tie and jacket, promptly fetched a silly tie and an outsized jacket and presented himself at the bar like Groucho Marx – an epitome of legal scruffiness) or whether it's our way of coping with the desperation of Sunday League cricket, but in stark contrast to yesterday's affable disinterestedness, today we were as full of life as dancers at a Mardi Gras.

They scored 158. It wasn't an important game to them and they rested Daniel, Cowans and Edmonds. Popplewell caught two stunning diving catches on the boundary, persuading Marks to sprint towards him like Superman. Botham said we were all being too quiet, which provoked a stream of remarks parodying gusto ('Well bowled, Bert', 'Great stop, Trev', 'Terrific stuff, Bill').

We won by four wickets after a mid-innings collapse. Lloyds and Slocombe had to repair the damage and I lounged in a bath while they were at work.

Middlesex 158 for 8, Somerset 159 for 6

Monday 22 August

v. Middlesex at Lord's (2nd day)
I retired hurt. Wayne Daniel's final delivery jumped off the Lord's ridge and hit my right thumb, making an unappetising mess of the top of the nail. I took off my glove, observed the damage and marched from the field to see Lord's blind physiotherapist. He felt the injury, realised that the nail and most of the matter under it were hanging forward and promptly snapped the nail back on to the thumb. This caused

a sudden and unexpected sharp pain and I will not repeat my cry. I was given pain-killer pills, though Falstaff said a bottle of brandy would be better, and was told to lie down since I would feel nauseous. Half an hour later a thunderstorm came up against the wind to flood Lord's, a turn of events which brought immense relief to the Somerset dressing room where people stopped watching St Trinians on television and went outside to watch the rain. Suddenly our balcony was full of white-clothed figures happily staring at the splashing men spreading hoses. Lord's was awash within minutes, though much of the rain slipped down the deep cracks caused by the heat of this dry summer.

It was with some amusement that we learnt that the Long Room had been flooded too.

At 5 pm the game was abandoned for the day and I took my throbbing thumb back to the hotel for a pot of tea before driving to the National Theatre to see *You Can't Take It With You*, which was chaotically funny.

We must be playing too much cricket. When a supposedly vital game between two excellent teams is watched by hardly any of the players and when a thunderstorm is greeted with wild good humour, something must be wrong with our system.

Somerset 249 and 72 for 1, Middlesex 242

Tuesday 23 August
v. Middlesex at Lord's (3rd day)
Thumb sore. Took no part in the game, which we won on a rain-affected pitch. Heathcliff bowled them out.

I was due for a rest tomorrow anyway, but as it is I'm injured and hoping to be fit for Saturday's match.

Somerset 249 and 119, Middlesex 242 and 93

Saturday 27 August
v. Glamorgan at Taunton (1st day)
Popplewell brought in a box of marrows this morning which he'd grown in his back garden. He gave them out to his team-mates. Gard spent most of the day talking about ferrets and shooting. Dredge had driven in from Frome, an hour away,

where he lives to be near his clan. Denning said he'd been to
see a tractor show yesterday.

These are the people who play cricket. Somehow an image
has grown of cricketers as greedy fellows who frequent night
clubs, pick up beautiful young ladies and dash about like
prima donnas in their sponsored cars. There aren't many of
those about. Ollis drives lorries for his Dad's firm in the
winter. Felton is a Cockney who is 'studying' at
Loughborough. Slocombe runs an antique shop, Marks
strives to do *The Times* crossword, Davis works on a building
site during the winter, Rose grows flowers and plays golf. You
know what Botham does. None of them fits that shallow
image.

Who else is there? Well, Richards is resting today and says
he might go along to the Notting Hill carnival. Hallam
Moseley has disappeared to London, where he is no doubt
happily cooking, cleaning and chatting patiently to whoever
turns up. Garner had to play today, forced to do so by my plea
that our bowling would be too weak without him; he'd
planned to spend a few days entertaining a family who'd
arrived to stay at his home.

It's a relief to have Garner in the team. As I announced our
XI to Mike Selvey (yes, I'm captain again), I saved his name to
last, knowing that Glamorgan had assumed that he was away
since he'd not been sighted yet. When I said, 'Oh yes, and
Garner,' I could almost feel Selvey's optimism fade and I
could anticipate how this surprising news would be received in
the Glamorgan dressing room.

We bowled them out for 218 and are 37 for 0 in reply. I was
nearly caught for 0. Still wary of my thumb, I tensed up at the
sight of a bumper and fended it off to short leg, who promptly
dropped it. After that I managed to be less of a pansy and
survived. It'll be a tight game because this pitch is helping the
bowlers.

Glamorgan 218, Somerset 37 for 0

Sunday 28 August

JPL v. Kent at Taunton
It's inevitable, I suppose, that if you are low in the
Championship and high in the Sunday League, you will

become something of a Jekyll and Hyde team. At any rate today we were sufficiently committed to argue with each other; you don't do that unless you care. In the end we battled our way to victory, surviving all our mistakes in the field. We won because Denning and I added 90 to set the scene for Richards, and because Richards furiously hit us to victory.

Our poor show on the field was caused simply by bad cricket, not through any panic. Kent, by contrast, tried too hard when we batted and gave us overthrows and wides. It was obvious that they were desperate to win, much as we had been in 1978. In fact they reminded me uncannily of us five years ago. We too had a burden of history hanging over us; like us, this Kent team has grown up together and their bonds are strong. It is ironic that their historic burden is one of success, whereas ours was one of failure. Today they fought almost too hard to show that they stood comparison with the great Kent teams of the past. Their ambition lent them a freshness of purpose that we lost when we won that first trophy in 1979.

Incidentally, what a remarkable difference wind makes to cricket. No wonder Boycott hangs out a handkerchief as he walks in to bat. Today the bowlers at one end were running into a gusty wind which pushed them off-balance and also helped the batsmen to drive. Even the fastest man bowling into the wind scarcely needed anyone behind square – the ball simply did not go there – whereas downwind bowlers needed most of their men behind square.

Marks and I first discovered the significance of wind when we were playing for Somerset against New Zealand years ago. A roly-poly man called McIntyre was bowling into the wind and Vic said that if anyone could hit the ball into the air it was bound to go for six. He said a spinner could hardly bowl into the wind at Taunton with short boundaries behind him. In went Vic to bat. To prove his point, he danced down the pitch to drive McIntyre up into the air. He missed the ball and was bowled. We didn't discuss the role of wind in cricket for some time to come after that.

Today's victory takes us to second in the League, behind the dreaded Yorkshire. If we win our last two games the title is ours. We've been second in the League five times in the last nine years, beaten by the arbitrary away wins rule.

Kent 221 for 7, Somerset 224 for 4

Monday 29 August
v. Glamorgan at Taunton (2nd day)
Alan Wilkins made a mistake today. He bowled short to Big
Bird Garner, or so Garner thought. Joel regards it as a
bowler's duty to deliver half-volleys to him and any ball
rising towards his ribs brings admonishing glares. Garner's
technique is to plunge forward every ball, his bat sweeping
through a long and unchanging course from shoulder to
shoulder. The line through which the bat swings is chosen
very early in proceedings so that if the ball deviates it is
missed. Accordingly, leg-spinners, left-arm spinners and
away-swingers trouble Garner as flies trouble cows: he cannot
quite get at them. On the other hand, inswingers or off-
spinners angling into his bat are scythed. Wilkins bowls
inswingers and had seen Garner score a hundred at Bristol. If
he pitched up he would be swept into the churchyard. So he
dropped a yard short, a perfectly reasonable tactic.

Garner didn't see things that way at all.

As it happens, I bumped into Wilkins in the car park. He'd
compounded his error by coming in as night-watchman, so
he'll be facing a fresh Garner in the morning. I told him
Garner was not pleased and said it should be an interesting
morning's cricket. If this doesn't put the fear of God into
Alan, nothing will.

This brief interlude brightened up a hard, grafting day's
cricket. I was out to Selvey, caught at slip foolishly pushing at
an away-swinger. We only approached their total by dint of
some huge blows by Garner and some rustic hits by Marks.
This evening Alan Jones, in his forty-fourth year and final
season of first-class cricket, played yet another marvellous
innings, dashing down the pitch to lift Marks over mid-
wicket. After tea we worked out a tactic to restrain him:
Marks bowled outside the off stump, forcing him to hit into
the covers. Spinners usually bowl at the stumps these days,
whereas they used to bowl outside the off stump, letting the
batsman drive and hoping for a catch in the covers or an edge.
Now the idea is to restrain the batsman and to force him to hit
against the spin. Alan Jones is very good at hitting off-spinners
against the spin to leg – he's been doing it for 27 years – and
it was just as well we tried something different.

Glamorgan 218 and 160 for 4, Somerset 214

Tuesday 30 August
v. Glamorgan at Taunton (3rd day)
A highly exciting victory was gained when Marks hooked
Winston Davis to the boundary. He and Garner hit the
winning runs, with Garner batting in a helmet for the first
time. Davis had bowled a fast spell, peppering the batsmen
with bumpers. There's only supposed to be one bumper an
over but this rule is not stringently applied. Consequently
batsmen were ducking and weaving for their lives as ball after
ball flew past. It was all hostile and tense, and both Marks and
Garner survived appeals for catches behind the wicket amidst
the clamour. Garner even played a back-foot shot for the first
time ever, hooking Wilkins out of the ground.

It occurs to me that during these three days I haven't talked
to my opposing captain, Mike Selvey, at all. I don't think
there is any grudge: he is probably one of those fellows who
get very het up during a day's cricket and like to drift away
on his own of an evening.

Viv was funny today (apart, I mean, from finding out that
he had to take care of his baby daughter for the day, at the end
of which he enigmatically gasped, 'I understand a lot now'),
rattling on about how the Welsh kept turning up with another
little square fellow with a moustache. We suggested, none too
convincingly, that the squatness was caused by the ancestors
being brought up in the mines, but we couldn't explain the
moustaches.

I think I'm captain again tomorrow. Popplewell is desperate
for a rest, his face white and drawn with match exhaustion.
But I don't think he's going to get a break. Garner wants a
game off before the final. Botham and Richards intend to relax
so that we are without Botham, Garner, Richards, Moseley
and Wilson, leaving only the ever-dependable Dredge to bowl
seamers. We need Popplewell's medium-pacers. I don't think
Nigel is going to be terribly pleased when I tell him he has to
play tomorrow.

Glamorgan 218 and 236, Somerset 214 for 7

Wednesday 31 August
v. Hampshire at Taunton (1st day)
Today's cricket was played in an extraordinary atmosphere.
Luckily, since Garner wasn't playing, the pitch was slow and

low — just the sort to frustrate Marshall, who bowled only seven overs this morning. Such was the mood of the game that when we agreed to bat on this evening in bad light, Marshall asked if he could bowl some leg-breakers. I replied that he couldn't bowl at all because he might slip a quick one in!

Hampshire bowled their spinners almost all day. Cowley, as bearded and genial as Marks, bowled his off-breaks and Chris Smith rolled up his lobs. I was embarrassed facing Smith because I could not wallop him as uninhibitedly, as, say, Botham would have done. He bowled nearly as slow as Norman Teer (see *Slices of Cricket*). At one stage I asked Pocock to give Marshall a bowl as at least I might look as if I could bat facing him.

It was at this stage that umpire Roy Palmer added to the merriment by throwing away all his spare balls. Obviously he reckoned he needn't carry any with Denning and me in — Denning isn't much cop at straight sixes either.

And then — well actually it was a couple of hours later — I went down the pitch and lifted Cowley back over his head. It went over the River Stand and into the Tone. I've never hit a ball into the river before. It was great fun.

I scored a century. It was not a difficult task in these almost light-hearted circumstances, though when I cut Smith past slip for two I did feel a deep surge of relief, as if I'd done something important. I ended up on 106 not out, an undistinguished innings apart from that one six. Is that all there is to scoring centuries? I feel no great sense of achievement, it was such a relaxed day, and my batting against Smith was so feeble that I could feel pleased but not proud. It was an innings played against some rice pudding bowling on a blancmange pitch.

At the end of this eerie day's cricket, an important one for Hampshire, who are third in the Championship, thunder and lightning is flashing around Taunton, giving us hope that we won't have to endure two more days of this.

Oh, by the way, I batted no. 4 today. It was like being moved from the front line of the trenches to the reserves miles behind.

Somerset 321 for 6

Thursday 1 September
v. Hampshire at Taunton (2nd day)
Two days to go before our Lord's final and here we are on another showery day in front of a few dozen people. It rained most of the morning but our ground is a notoriously quick dryer and was playable again at 2 pm.

It was interesting to watch Chris Smith trying to coax his mind into activity before play began. I was teasing Nick Pocock that we were going to bat on and Chris Smith approached me with half an hour to go, asking whether we had declared. I said we had, whereupon Smith ran a few laps of the barren ground, stretched his muscles and then put on his pads for some practice. He's scored 1750 first-class runs this year and lots in overs games too, as well as representing England, but nevertheless he wants to score more, partly to secure his tour place and partly to reach 2000 runs. So there he was, trying to defy the banality of the day. Pocock said Smith had 'Gone over the top' as horses do, and added that however much he cajoled himself, he was bound to make mistakes.

Smith scored 20 or so in a grisly innings; you could see he was fed up with his poor timing and form. He was out bowled by Lloyds, inaccurately trying to cover-drive. He might have been better off playing like everyone else today, in a breezy vein. But then I suppose that his success has been based on concentration; like Boycott, he's a day in, day out man.

Gordon Greenidge hit 70 today but could have been out first ball. I'd just set the field and settled down for a trying afternoon at gully, happy in the thought that the pitch was a beauty and that nothing would whizz my way. Then Dredge somehow produced a wicked lifter that hit Greenidge's bat handle and flew behind me. I scurried back but could not quite get to it. A colleague said that milk turned quicker.

After Pocock's declaration we lost three wickets, one of them Felton to a silly swipe. He apologised later but I told him I'd once heard Alan Jones say, 'Apologise before you do it, then don't do it.' I'm 6 not out. Two more days until our cup final and still it's just another game to me. It must be the weather dampening the spirit and dampening enthusiasm.

This has been so far an appalling though good-tempered game. The statistics in the paper seem so irrelevant, failing to capture the realities of this match.

Somerset 321 for 6 dec. and 47 for 3, Hampshire 253 for 3 dec.

Friday 2 September

v. Hampshire at Taunton (3rd day)

Lunchtime. This is demented. Sitting in the dressing room having just downed plaice and chips with sherry trifle to follow, listening to the gales howl outside and hoping that the clouds bring some rain. We are playing and I'm 17 not out. The bails won't stay on and you can't hear your partner call and there only ten people sitting in the River Stand in an otherwise deserted ground. What an extraordinary ritual this is, with Malcolm Marshall pounding them down at full throttle. I find it an immense challenge to my professionalism, not to say greed for runs, to commit myself totally to a job on days like this.

2.45. All out 86! We were 67 for 4 at lunch then I was out for 20, brilliantly caught at leg slip. Can't understand how the ball went to leg slip. There was a gusty cross-wind which must have blown the ball across me as I was trying to on-drive. I took my pads off, stirred a cup of coffee and sat down to watch the fellows fight it out. Marshall took four wickets in five balls and that was the end of my cup of coffee!

Now we are to go into the field, except that a shower has held up play. The sight-screens have blown over and the rain is stopping, which adds to our damp depression. This day seems as if it will never end. Nello (our Italian supporter — in Somerset even the Italians follow cricket) and Falstaff are here but apart from that it's a miserable scene.

8.45 pm. in London. Sitting alone in my little Italian restaurant, watching torrential rain pour down and wondering if we'll play our cup final tomorrow. I hope we do; a rainy day would spoil tomorrow's festivities. I feel as dead as I did for the semi-final; I've been stumbling along from day to day with scarcely a thought for this supposedly vital game. It was only as we approached London that I began to wake up. As we splashed through puddles I began to feel edgy, bad-tempered even. Tomorrow I must ply my trade in front of tens of thousands of people, just me against 11 of them, watched by millions on television.

It will be a dramatic change from the horrors of today to the hopes of tomorrow. What an extraordinary preparation these last few days have been. After the winds and the hard grind I feel like a war veteran, and have hardly any resources of patience or toleration left for tomorrow. These last three days in particular, with our ground as abandoned as a derelict airport, have left us flat, frustrated, unexcited.

Botham has called a meeting for this evening at 9.45 to discuss the game. Our meetings have never made a scrap of difference before. We don't so much prepare as arrive. I think our attitude is 'Let the opposition worry about us, we don't want to know anything at all about them.' Analysis can do harm sometimes. Before last season's Benson & Hedges Final I asked Garner what Hadlee bowled, as I'd never faced him, and he replied, 'He's as quick as me and moves the ball both ways!'

I wonder if Kent, in their first final, realise that we feel nearly as vulnerable as they do. Even our mighty players are conscious of their frailties.

Somerset 321 for 6 dec. and 86, Hants 253 for 3 dec. and 41 for 1

9

A Bang and a Whimper

Saturday 3 September

Natwest Bank Trophy Final v. Kent at Lord's
Let me remember as much of this drama as I can.

Last night's meeting was cancelled because Garner and
Denning arrived late at the hotel, having hijacked our ex-
Chairman who is on crutches and who hadn't planned to come
to the game. We sat around for an hour sipping lager, an
interlude which at least did no damage to our cause, and which
was brightened by Richards' news that his wife had given
birth to a boy. Richards asked me to hump through African
history books to find an ethnic name for his son.

I shared a room with Popplewell. We slept soundly, partly because the weather was foul and we didn't expect to play. Woke up at 7.30, had a slow breakfast and set off for Lord's at 8.40.

Arrived to find a deserted visitors' dressing room filled only by balloons and telegrams. There had been long lines of people waiting for the gates to open, and these provided the first inkling that the day would contrast sharply with yesterday's nonsense at Taunton.

I sat alone in our dressing room until 9.15 when 'Bilko' Waight arrived. We were supposed to be starting at 10.30 and stretching at 9.30, and I was annoyed that our kit had not arrived. And where the hell was the team? I wanted to prepare myself slowly and carefully in case we had to bat first. Sometimes if the toss is late, I strap on my pads and get ready just in case.

Eventually word arrived that the kit was ready for collection downstairs and gradually our room filled with a shrill jollity. Whether it was the weather or not I cannot say, but I still felt lacking in spark. I was still, absurdly, trying to generate a feverish and creative excitement as I strolled across the ground with Marks to practise at the nursery end. The game should have stirred me by then, yet I had no electricity.

Our routine was as scatty as usual. Vic rolled down a few off-breaks to me which I hit, and then I trundled a few half-volleys to him which he drove. After that we caught a few slip catches, did our stretches with Bilko and then at 10 am pottered back to the pavilion for a cup of tea as if it were any other day.

I sat in the dressing room quietly, with only a few officials around and John Cleese, whom we'd invited to share our day with us (he is a genuine Somerset cricket man). Other players returned gradually and news spread that the start had been delayed. It emerged that this was a ploy by the umpires, who believed that a 60-over game could not be finished on a day like this whereas a 50-over match starting at 11 am might.

At 10.30 Botham went out to toss. I changed into my batting gear, trying to encourage the coin to fall our way so that we could field. I know it doesn't do any bloody good – I'm not an idiot, you know! Immediately after the toss, the cameras and Peter West swooped in on Tavaré, who evidently had won the toss. He'd certainly put us in to bat on so mucky a day and on so green a pitch.

This change to a 50-over game was unsettling. 50-overs is such an awkward length. Do you play it like a 60-over match, for the most part of which you bat only slightly more adventurously than you do in a Championship game? Or do you play in more cavalier style as you would in a 40-over game in which scarcely a ball is left alone? I've never played in a 50-over game before. Would they try to bowl us out or to contain us?

We soon had our answer. Denning and I arrived in the middle, followed by the roars of supporters; to find a moist, green pitch and a string of slips. Dilley's first over was fast, delivered from the pervading gloom of the dark windows and red bricks of the pavilion end. One ball rose sharply and stung Denning's wrist. Each ball made a red mark on the surface as moisture encouraged movement. Both Denning and I contrived to squeeze a single in that first over, his to mid-wicket, mine past fourth slip.

Ellison opened at the other end with away-swingers into the wind. I drove his first ball past cover for four. Next ball I punished to mid-off where Underwood made a diving stop. Next ball I drove again and it flashed past third slip to the boundary. I tried to push the fourth ball to leg; it started around leg stump, swung viciously across and missed off stump. This brought my essay into flashing drives to an abrupt end. What on earth had my body been up to? Why was I playing so loosely? I could not find a reason except that my nerves must have been so pumped up that no amount of restraint could work.

At the end of that over Denning asked me if I was going for the fastest fifty or something. Sadly, he was trapped lbw to Dilley almost immediately. He is conscious that he has a poor record in finals at Lord's and feels a burden because of this as if he owed the team some runs. Everyone else regards it as just one of those inexplicable things; it is the pressure we put on ourselves that makes life difficult.

I was out in the fifth over, bowled Dilley for 11. It was a full-length straight ball which simply eluded my forward push. As it hurtled towards me I wanted to drive it past the bowler for one or two. I felt my back foot slip slightly, pushing me off-balance, and the ball darted through a gap between bat and pad which isn't usually there. Apart from the slip I was beaten by pace; I simply didn't find time to make all the manoeuvres I'd intended. I suppose I turned a full-length ball into a yorker.

I heard the ball hit the stumps with a dull thud and for a moment there was silence, which annoyed me. Didn't it matter that I was out? Where were the oohs of our supporters and the roars of theirs? A moment later a burst of noise broke, and off I went towards the pavilion without looking back to study the damage.

There were a few quiet 'bad luck's' in our room but no-one said much, least of all me. There was nothing much to say. I'd missed the ruddy thing and that was that. It's not often I'm out to that sort of technical mistake. I really couldn't work it out.

Surprisingly, I recovered quickly. It can be almost a relief to be out of the melting pot, though this doesn't mean you hide when you're in it. I changed into a track-suit and chatted on our balcony to John Cleese and our President, Colin Atkinson, while the game unfolded before us. It was subdued cricket, I suppose because of the damp weather and the slow scoring. It wasn't a pitch upon which Slocombe and Richards could dominate, and the duels were tense rather than thrilling. Richards did hit one ball in the air straight between two fieldsmen. As he hit the shot we held our breath, sighing when we saw it flash to the boundary. If Richards hit 100, that moment of luck would be forgotten, yet he could have been out. In all of his triumphant innings Richards would readily concede that he could have failed.

Slocombe was out for a valuable 20 and on the stroke of lunch Richards was caught behind, cutting at Dilley. I went straight upstairs to have some meat and vegetables and so missed any mood of dejection in our room. It was quiet, though, when I returned half an hour later. Apparently this silence had prevailed the whole time, as if our hopes had suffered an unexpected blow when we were most vulnerable. I expect soccer teams find this if they concede a goal just before half-time.

After lunch we fought on, though Botham was quickly caught. Perhaps he, too, tried too hard, reining in his prodigious hitting in an effort to play a substantial innings. Popplewell stayed almost to the end, picking up runs where he could, and Marks played perhaps the only flighty innings of the match in clubbing 26 in the final few overs. We reached 193 for 9, not too bad a score in the prevailing conditions.

Between innings I popped into the gents behind our dressing room. There is no privacy at Lord's. Where you wander, so do lots of men in MCC ties. In the gents you find yourself surrounded by many members attending to their business. I wonder if this happens at Wembley, this close relationship between actor and audience? I could think of no other cricket ground where we all share the same gents.

It was only as we strode onto the field that I felt a surge of tension for the first time. At last, in response to the urgencies of the day, I felt my sardonic façade slip away. I regretted that I had not felt so alive with the bat either in the semi-final or the final. When Garner took an early wicket, I rushed up from long leg to join in the celebrations. And when Richards dropped Tavaré I heard myself shout, 'Oh no, Viv', not that anyone could hear anything in the din. I could make my comments out loud, secure in the knowledge that they'd be lost in the understanding air.

Rain forced an early tea but not before our West Indians had dropped more catches. I'd heard that Richards had been disturbed in the night by an urgent phone call from Taunton Hospital, asking permission to operate on his wife. He hadn't mentioned this to anyone – he doesn't make excuses.

Popplewell had bowled three leg-side half-volleys to Tavaré in one over and we were in trouble. During the interval Popplewell's Dad (a judge, and evidently a good judge) popped in to suggest to his son that leg-side half-volleys were not the thing to bowl to Tavaré. 'Falstaff' McCombe, sensing the gloomy atmosphere, asked if he should do a striptease to cheer everyone up, and Marks said that if they lost a couple of wickets they might panic. This was, after all, their first final. This interval turned the game. It disturbed Kent's momentum and stopped our sulking. We realised, sat in chairs, that they were only 46 for 1 in 18 overs, a cold statistic which denied the drift of the game as it had been flowing in the field. They were on a winning run but the run had not yet reached its fulfilment.

Botham said he was going to bowl Richards and Marks and stuff the pitch, which was supposed to be helping the seamers.

Richards pinned down Tavaré and Johnson, forcing them to risk all against Marks. Both these bowlers tested the nerve of the batsmen, stopping their easy runs and inviting them to go over the top if they dared. Johnson swung wildly at Marks and was bowled, and shortly afterwards Tavaré drove Marks hard and low to deep mid-wicket. Guess who was there? As the ball hurtled towards me, I can remember thinking, 'Oh my God, I must catch this.' I lost the ball against the Mound Stand but picked it up again rifling straight at me. I put up my hands and felt the ball sink into my right hand. It could have slipped out. I waited for an instant, found the ball still there and tossed it into the air thinking, 'Good God, I've caught Tavaré.' I saw Richards and others charging across and I tried to look as nonchalant as possible.

Kent quickly lost two more wickets, both to excellent stumpings by Gard, for whom the day must have been traumatic. He'd waited for years in Taylor's shadow, scarcely ever playing because Taylor rarely suffered any injuries, but suddenly here he was in his first full season, playing in a Lord's final. After his stumpings he jumped into Botham's arms, intoxicated with relief.

Just as we were about to finish them off, another spurt of rain help up play and we repaired to our much more noisy dressing room. But the brief delay not only stopped the tide of affairs but turned them agonisingly in Kent's favour. Perhaps we had swung from depression to over-confidence, forgetting how astonishingly fragile is ascendancy in sport.

Shortly after play resumed, Eldine Baptiste was bowled and then Knott skied a hit to deep mid-on. Well now, see if you can guess who was under the ball at deep mid-on? As it fell towards me, I hoped desperately to hear some colleague cry 'mine!' No such luck, and I realised if I dropped this one there would be loud, ironic, embarrassing cheers. I caught it, then turned to hold up the ball for the crowd to see.

We thought Kent were finished. We were wrong. Ellison and Dilley hit out, clouting Dredge over mid-wicket, over cover and straight. Richards was furious that Dredge could not pitch yorkers on leg stump. I expect he was trying to, but the strain in these situations is immense. Suddenly they wanted 42 in 8 overs with three wickets in hand. But if a wicket fell there was only Underwood and Jarvis to come. Jarvis is a real tail-ender. He's only ever hit one six in first-class cricket – and guess who the bowler was!

Ellison was hit on the knee by Garner, steaming in from the darker pavilion end. That pretty well ended Kent's hopes, for Ellison couldr.'t bat properly any longer and needed a runner. Dilley backed away to slash Garner, missed and was bowled. Two overs later Ellison made the same mistake – rather unnecessarily, I thought. They could have taken their chances at the other end and blocked Garner. It's easy to see that when it isn't you involved. The cup was ours when Botham caught Jarvis and as we rushed from the field, I grabbed a stump for Falstaff and beat my way through people hurtling in all directions.

The champagne was already open in the dressing room and I picked up a glass and sat quietly in my corner. I felt more immediately happy than after previous finals, presumably because I'd been less wound up before the game so that relaxation came more readily. Trevor Gard was in tears, a reaction to his emotional effort during the day. Our room quickly filled up with officials, colonels and noisy exuberance. Botham took us out to listen to the speeches and collect our medals. Tavaré offered his congratulations and the Kent fellows put on a brave face. They sent a crate of champagne to our dressing room and came over to share it. We went back to our dressing room and I sat chatting to Marks and Aslett and whoever else slipped into our group, hardly aware of the noisy clamour. The next hour and a half passed in a blur of conversations drowned by the rising tide of noise, chatting about the game and experiences in professional cricket.

At last people drifted away and only a few players were left. At nine I finally undressed and had a shower. Richards and Botham had not changed yet: they are always last to leave, avoiding autograph hunters and lingering in what is, after all, their empire.

Finally, at 9.30, into a car and off to Worcester, stopping along the way for a pint and a hot dog. Is that how champions are supposed to celebrate? Arrived in Worcester at midnight and sat in the bar for half an hour, rummaging through the day's events. Some of the players probably stayed up later than me.

Somerset 193 for 9, Kent 169

Sunday 4 September

JPL v. Worcestershire at Worcester
It's a pity that the Natwest Trophy Final isn't the last game of the season. We had no time to recover from its highly charged emotions and whereas the young Worcester team had obviously been building themselves up for this game, we were very flat. At its end they jumped up and down, hurtled from the field with huge grins on their faces and dashed into their dressing room to celebrate. And all their victory does is lift them a couple of places up the table. We merely changed slowly and wandered across for a drink with the sponsors before motoring home. A couple of friends of mine turned up and we sat on the grass sipping wine and chatting outside the tent; we'd been there for an hour before the first Worcester players arrived, evidently having taken a long time to unwind from their rare win.

We were sluggish in the field, especially those for whom yesterday's final was a fresh experience. I suppose people will think this was because of undue celebrations last night. Our team doesn't consist of archangels at the best of times, but nothing untoward happened. We lost because we misread the pitch, because Collis King turned up and lashed 48 and because we simply didn't play well. It happens.

Worcs 192, Somerset 137

Saturday 10 September

v. Warwickshire at Taunton (1st day)
Back after a few days off. I didn't play against Kent on Wednesday because there didn't seem much point, and anyway it was a chance to give experience to some youngsters.

It was a cold, windy end to the season. Autumn is upon us with its skidding clouds and sudden showers of rain. There was dew on the grass this morning and Gordon Prossor said, 'There's been the first frost of the season today.' The cricket was only of slight interest to its players. We did play a bit between the showers but even when the game was in progress, most cricketers watched television or played cards. It was as if the last rites are being performed and cold statistics collected.

Warwickshire are high in the Championship and they made us fight for our runs. I was out to a good ball early from Chris Old which lifted and left me. Shortly afterwards Old hobbled off with a sore knee. Gifford laid aside his beloved pipe to take his hundredth wicket of the season and Paul Smith steamed in with some hostile overs. Nevertheless Julian Wyatt, a farmer's son from Paulton, and Nigel Felton from Kent scored some excellent runs. Later, less seriously, Gard went in to bat with Lance Cairns' huge weapon. He couldn't pick up the thing but he survived as night-watchman. Perhaps that's why he survived. It was a mixed sort of a day.

Somerset 149 for 5

Sunday 11 September

JPL v. Warwickshire at Taunton
Morning. It's a miserable morning, cold, wet and windy. It seems as if we are to end the season as we began it.

If Yorkshire win or are rained off this afternoon, the Sunday title is theirs. If they lose and we win, it's ours. It's their first chance to win a trophy since 1969, whereas we have played so many big games these past few seasons that we treat them almost like any other day. The pressure is on them and they will be forever looking over their shoulders, hoping Somerset lose. We can simply enjoy ourselves, if enjoyment is possible on so unsympathetic a day.
Evening. In a sad anti-climax we won our game but Yorkshire were rained off and so we finished on equal points and they took the title on the away wins technicality. What is so noble about away wins for heaven's sake?

Seven thousand people packed our ground this afternoon, defying the wretched weather. It rained until noon and still they flocked to the ground. Perhaps the best thing about this club is the close atmosphere between supporters, groundsmen, caterers, barmen, cleaning ladies and secretaries. Everyone knows everyone else's name, there is no proud hierarchy. Now as winter sets in, many of the players will disappear and the supporters will hibernate, but the workers in the club will still be there every day. Like the players, they will quickly be bored by the emptiness of the ground and they will await the more exciting atmosphere of summer at the county ground.

Today's game was ill-tempered, a rather bitty game played with the constant worry that rain might fall at any moment. Once again our passive approach of yesterday (we did not bother to stretch) contrasted with our straining determination this afternoon. Every time a ball went into the outfield someone would urge the fieldsman to get it quickly and save runs. It was all so taut, with players on both teams living on the edge of their nerves.

They scored 170 or so and we lost early wickets (including Roebuck yorked by Smith, almost a repetition of my dismissal at Lord's) but Botham hit 49 and Marks smote 44. With steady rain falling, several players stood on the balcony trying to work out who was ahead on run-rate. Popplewell stormed around with a sheet of paper which would have explained everything if anyone could understand it. For some reason the team regarded me as the fountain of mathematical accuracy, but by the time I'd worked out whether we were ahead or behind, some idiot had scored another run. When it was obvious even to the naked mind that our rate was faster than theirs, Botham stood on the balcony and brought the heavy rain to the attention of the umpires, who started to leave the field. Some of the Warwickshire men stayed on, pointing out that it was only a shower and they could carry on, whereupon the umpires turned round and the game resumed, to our fury. But Garner hit some runs and we finished this acrimonious game as victors. The extraordinary thing about all this was that we knew Yorkshire had been rained off and were champions. Only pride was at stake this afternoon as it turned out. But perhaps pride is the sharpest weapon a team can have.

After the game the crowd called for Botham, who made some heroic speech about how we were going to win 'the bloody lot' next year, and although a party mood developed in the dressing room, I slipped away, saddened that the title had eluded us and not wanting to sit in a packed, noisy dressing room sipping beer after such a fraught day's cricket.

Our second place today brought us £6,500, or about £300 a man after tax.

Warwicks 174 for 7, Somerset 175 for 7

Monday 12 September

v. Warwickshire at Taunton (2nd day)
10.55 am. The five-minute bell has just been rung. A groundsman in a red track-suit is hurriedly painting white lines on the pitch. Two men in flat caps and raincoats are staring at the pitch. Around the ground there are a few people in ones and twos, sipping coffee and wondering why they are here.

The umpires are walking out to the square, followed by England's captain and his county team. It's a murky day. The kids are ready in the scoreboard, Eric Hill is at his post in the press box, the scorers are alert, the chef is busy preparing lunch and everything is set for the second last day of this season.
Night. The port was out at lunch and tea, handed around by Popplewell to bring warmth to cold bones. I didn't have any as I was acting captain (Botham was at a meeting). In the field I wore two vests, a shirt and two sweaters.

It was a day for the youngsters. Gary Palmer bowled them out and tonight we sent out Heathcliff and Julian Wyatt (who seems to enjoy batting) to survive the last few minutes.

One more day to go.

Somerset 219 and 0 for 0, Warwickshire 300 for 9 dec.

Tuesday 13 September

v. Warwickshire at Taunton (3rd day)
And so another season has drifted by. It scarcely seems six months ago that we gathered at Millfield and began our preparations. Eventually, I suppose, all the games will become confused in my mind. Was it this year or last that it rained all April? Was it this year or last that I couldn't catch up with the overs?

Already I am remembering particular moments rather than particular games, particular strokes rather than particular

..nings. I remember hitting the ball into the Tone for the first
.ime, I remember being out swiping for the first time in years,
I remember one marvellous stroke played through the leg-side
at Bath. I remember catching almost nothing in the slips and
almost everything in the outfield. We won a cup final at
Lord's but I look back with more affection upon our time
during the World Cup when we were a weak young team
doing its best. If I learnt anything this season, it is that the
pleasure of professional sport lies not in winning trophies but
in playing in a team when it is giving itself heart and soul to its
work.

Our scorer has presented us with our statistics of the
season. I avoided being caught quite so often, only 28 times
compared to 36. On the other hand I've been bowled 12 times,
run out 3 and lbw 7 times (according to the umpires at any
rate) and stumped only once. Apparently I batted for 1920
more minutes than anyone else in county games and scored
more slowly than anyone else except Richard Ollis.

If I dared to risk being stumped more often, perhaps I
would be more entertaining. After all, I went down the pitch
lots of times and missed only once. It's a good risk. Perhaps,
though, it's not in my nature. I was spurred on by fear of
dismissal and fear of failure. These affect my conduct much
more than any joy in hitting the ball or any love of success.

Of course these bare statistics hide as much as they reveal.
They did not mention those dreadfully long journeys or that
rude despondency in Manchester. They ignore the poignant
moments of laughter, they disdain the pressure and the
crowds. They do not show us the men.

We ended on a low note with the teams grumpily playing
out the last few hours after lunch with no pretence of pleasure.
Luckily a couple of our excellent young men, Wyatt (I think
we'll have to call him Earp) and Heathcliff, survived most of
the afternoon. Heathcliff defied his origins so far as to hit
Gifford for a straight six, doubling his tally of first-class runs.
I had to endure the final hour, defending against some
tantalising donkey-drops from Gifford, a duty performed
with as much devotion as I could muster.

Our last morning was much more entertaining. Upon
arriving at the ground I found a champagne breakfast in full
swing with Botham as Master of Ceremonies. It was pouring

down and everyone was quite sure we wouldn't have to pla
today. We sat around the table, sipping champagne for two
hours and talking jovially. It was only at 11.50 that I spotted
the form: the rain had nearly stopped and the clouds were
breaking up. I left the breakfast and repaired to the dressing
room, where some of our youngsters were already carefully
playing snooker. I stood under a cold shower and tried to read
the papers. I realised that we were likely to have to play later
in the day and I'd probably have to bat. I didn't want to ruin
my average. I wanted to give myself as much chance to do well
as possible. I was a dour professional right to the end.

Somerset 219 and 117 for 1, Warwicks 300 for 9 dec.

Wednesday 14 September

I had meant to end this diary as the season ended. There
didn't seem much point in observing the slow unwinding of
benefit matches and cocktail parties. But this morning we flew
up in an 11-seater to Newcastle (I wish I could capture the
studied concentration of Joel Garner as the pilot described
how to open the emergency door) and played a night game in
Northumberland.

I batted 'brilliantly' (I quote the local newspaper). I report
this with mixed emotions. There was scarcely any sense in
batting artistically in Newcastle on 14 September. It made me
wonder if I had not misused my talent. Tonight I hit straight
sixes, backed away to play some delicate late cuts and stepped
inside a left-arm spinner to lift him over cover. To be frank, I
played a stream of strokes of which I had not thought myself
capable. My century, in 84 balls against a competent attack
including a Jamaican opening bowler, astounded my team-
mates. Vic said he had no idea I could bat with such class and
why didn't I do it more often? I reflected that I'd never even
tried to bat like this before, never even given myself the
chance to play these shots.

Was it a freak? I cannot think so. For once I took my
courage in my hands and decided I was going to entertain the
crowd, not wait for Richards and Botham to do it. Perhaps the
insecurity of batting, sharpened as it is by being my career,
has caused me to concentrate on the avoidance of failure rather

than accepting the challenges. I wonder if I can still release those parts of my game which I had thought had long since vanished. To succeed in this I would have to be more tolerant of bad dismissals, I'd have to endure mishap with a shrug and a laugh. Probably I've been too intense about it all.

I must round off this postscript with a few details.

Joel Garner is not touring this winter with the West Indies but is resting at home with his sore shoulder. He averaged 26.5 as a batsman for Somerset, a substantial improvement on previous efforts. I don't think you could say he'd altogether 'done swipin'', though.

Richards is in India and Botham and Marks are to go to Pakistan in the New Year. Falstaff is battening down for the winter and Heathcliff has disappeared back to the Yorkshire moors from whence he came. Popplewell is teaching in Taunton and Denning and Dredge and the others are around somewhere, though I doubt if any of us will see each other before 5 April 1984.

I'm off to teach in Australia. I won't keep a diary there. There really is no need.